The Fruit of Her Hands

The Fruit of Her Hands

A PSYCHOLOGY OF
BIBLICAL WOMAN

Matthew B. Schwartz *and* Kalman J. Kaplan

WILLIAM B. EERDMANS PUBLISHING COMPANY
GRAND RAPIDS, MICHIGAN / CAMBRIDGE, U.K.

Published 2007 by
Wm. B. Eerdmans Publishing Co.
2140 Oak Industrial Drive N.E., Grand Rapids, Michigan 49505 /
P.O. Box 163, Cambridge CB3 9PU U.K.

Printed in the United States of America

12 11 10 09 08 07   7 6 5 4 3 2 1

Library of Congress Cataloging-in-Publication Data

Schwartz, Matthew B.
The fruit of her hands: a psychology of biblical woman /
Matthew B. Schwartz and Kalman J. Kaplan.
p.   cm.
Includes bibliographical references.
ISBN 978-0-8028-1772-3 (pbk.: alk. paper)
1. Women in the Bible. 2. Bible. O.T. — Psychology.
I. Kaplan, Kalman J.   II. Title.

BS1199.W7S93   2007
221.8′155333 — dc22

2006103520

www.eerdmans.com

To the biblical women in our families —
past, present, and future

Contents

CONTENTS

Contents

Acknowledgments

Heather Shirk's personal encouragement to the authors and her technical skill in preparing the manuscript have been invaluable. We are grateful to Professors Laura Kline and Guy Stern of Wayne State University, and Kitty Allen of the Southfield (Michigan) Library, who have shared with us of their wonderful knowledge of literature.

Reinder Van Til is a gem among editors, himself an experienced author, knowledgeable, clearheaded, dedicated, and a master of his craft. To Mr. William Eerdmans, to Reinder, Jenny Hoffman, Justin Lawrence, and all the staff at Eerdmans — our warmest thanks.

Finally, Dr. Kaplan would like to thank Gary Garrison of the Fulbright Foundation and Dr. Neal Sherman and Judy Stavsky of the United States–Israel Education Foundation and David Goldberg for providing the funds to allow the completion of this project.

Dr. Kaplan would also like to thank his hosts at Tel Aviv University, Professors Daniel Algom, Amiram Raviv, and Giora Kienan of the Department of Psychology and Professor Shlomo Shoham of The Buchman School of Law, for providing the facilities to do the editing of this work, and to the alert, engaging, and always questioning students and friends at Tel Aviv University, especially the biblical women among them.

CHAPTER I

The Greek Model

The Western literary tradition offers a large number of very unhappy heroines. They seem to measure themselves in terms of their success with men — be it fathers, husbands, lovers, or sons — but they rarely have healthy or satisfying relations with those men. Their native gifts and talents do not develop, nor do their characters, and their ends are predictably tragic. They are angry with others and unhappy that they are women. Consider a few examples.

(1) Emma Bovary, the central figure of Gustave Flaubert's great novel *Madame Bovary,* interests herself in a series of men, especially Rodolphe, with whom she carries on a lengthy affair. The wife of a small-town doctor, Emma has no interest in either her husband, Charles, or her young daughter, both of whom dote on her. She dreams about the exciting narratives she reads in her novels, and she expects her affairs to add a sentimental and passionate color to what she regards as her drab life. Emma spends irresponsibly and lies to her husband about it. She confuses sensual luxury with true joy, elegance and manners with true feeling. All this ends in a way that the reader can almost predict — though Emma, apparently, cannot. Her life unravels, leading to her suicide; her husband's death comes not long afterward. Emma is, at her core, a confused woman who does not know right from wrong and who lacks the strength or sense of purpose to give any value to her life.

(2) In Henrik Ibsen's *A Doll's House,* Nora is another female character whose life has been defined largely by unhealthy relationships with both her husband and father, and she is unable to overcome their infantilizing of her. In many ways a devoted and resourceful person, she nonetheless takes on the role of an irresponsible and child-like doll in her relationship with her husband, Torvald. He, in turn, calls her his "little skylark" and "a spendthrift," and he chides her for constantly wheedling him for money because she is so financially irresponsible. The fact is, however, that Nora is acting very responsibly within the constraints of her husband's attitude.

Early in their marriage Torvald had become sick from overworking, and his physician had informed Nora that he would die unless he could go south for an extended rest. The trip had been expensive, and Torvald assumed that Nora had received the money for it from her dying father. However, Nora's father had not given her the money. Unbeknownst to Torvald, she had taken out a loan from a banker to finance what turned out to be a yearlong rest in Italy. The rest has saved Torvald's life, and Nora is justifiably proud of that. But she has been paying the loan back with money she gets from her husband by pretending to be extravagant and irresponsible — the "spendthrift."

To make matters worse, Nora has secured the loan with a bond on which she has forged her father's signature at the time of his death. When the creditor is threatened with losing his job at Torvald's bank, he tries to blackmail Nora into putting pressure on Torvald to keep him by threatening to inform her husband of this forgery. Inevitably, Nora fails to influence her husband, the creditor loses his job, and the latter carries out his threat to inform Torvald. Upon receiving the information, Torvald flies into a rage, condemning and rejecting Nora. He informs her that they must stay together for appearances' sake, but that she will no longer be his wife or have any role in raising their children. At this point, Nora realizes who this person to whom she has been married really is.

Soon afterwards, the creditor has a change of heart and returns the bond to Torvald, who immediately changes his tune: he says that he realizes that Nora's actions were motivated by love for him, and he forgives her for her behavior. But it's too late. Nora says that she has been married to a stranger and announces that she will leave him and even her children in an attempt to find herself. She will thus also escape her relationships with the men who infantilize her.

There is no question that Ibsen's Nora has been wronged: she is unappreciated and abandoned by her husband; indeed, she has been misunderstood and demeaned by her father years before. Torvald's actions show him to be a man who has little use for women. Though Nora is quite resourceful and shows a capacity for being a healthy partner, she has been emotionally abandoned by her partner at a critical juncture in her life. Making the stark choice between herself and her family, she ultimately flies away to find herself, thus ironically becoming the "little skylark" her husband has labeled her out of his own blindness.

(3) Arguably one of the greatest of novels by one of the greatest of novelists is *Anna Karenina* by Leo Tolstoy. Anna, a charming and beautiful woman, runs away with Count Vronsky, leaving behind her husband and young son and causing them great pain. Tolstoy's characters are multidimensional, but Anna seems to find her life's main interest in working her charms on strange men. Levin is portrayed as a good man who feels drawn to Anna's charm even in the downward days of her life. Finally, impelled by her failure to attain supreme happiness with Vronsky, and also by her drugs, Anna throws herself to her death under a train. Despite certain obvious abilities, Anna seems unable to develop deeper relationships with men and to live according to any purpose beyond her distorted search for flirtation. Another female character, Kitty, goes into a deep depression after losing Vronsky to Anna, but she is able to learn to love others and to recognize the spiritual in life. She marries Levin, and though there are gaps in their togetherness, she understands and supports him in his own search for meaning. Levin, in turn, appreciates Kitty's kindness and insight; it is a marriage in which both partners can work and grow.

(4) Another great Russian writer, Anton Chekhov, in his short story "Anna on the Neck," portrays an eighteen-year-old girl who marries a prosperous fifty-two-year-old government official to salvage

her drunken schoolteacher father and her two little brothers. She must play up to the wives of other officials in order to further her husband's career, while he gives her some jewelry but little money. Finally, Anna attends a ball in a new dress, and she is greatly admired. From that time on, visitors often come to call on her, and she says to her husband, "Be off, you blockhead." Anna is never without a picnic or play to attend, and she spends her husband's money as she wills, paying no further attention to him or, indeed, to her father and brothers. In the end, Anna becomes exactly the kind of person for whom she has always felt a mixture of envy and contempt.

(5) Edith Wharton's *House of Mirth* is a fin-de-siècle novel that focuses on Lily Barth, a beautiful and intelligent woman whose family has lost its money. She associates with and flirts with a series of men, hoping to recover from her financial ruin by entering a wealthy marriage. In doing so, she passes up Lawrence Selden, who is interested in her in a deeper way but who, she feels, is less likely to bring her into higher society. Despite having certain appealing characteristics, Lily becomes just another fictional woman who goes downhill to her tragic death.

(6) One of Germany's greatest novelists, Theodor Fontane, wrote a novel entitled *Effi Briest* (1895). Effi is a warm and attractive personality who marries the former suitor of her mother, a man too old and straitlaced for her. Her dissatisfaction leads her to have an affair with Major Crampas, who plays on her weaknesses and is contemptuous of her husband. But Effi, feeling deeply guilty, finally ends her affair with Crampas and returns to her husband. Seven years later, however, her husband learns of the affair and totally rejects Effi (and subsequently kills Crampas in a duel). Cut off from her child and from the regularity of her former life, Effi deteriorates and finally dies. She seems to have allowed the whole progression of her life to depend on what her husband thinks of her — or does not think of her. A mere adolescent at the beginning of the story, she is not prepared for responsibilities, and she can also be deceptive. Effi's husband certainly does lack warmth; but Effi, rather than addressing the problem, chooses to engage in an affair. Bright and in some ways likable, Effi has no purpose or motivation beyond relieving the pain of her situation.

ALL THESE FICTIONAL HEROINES of the Western literary tradition suffer from an inability to integrate what psychologists call individuation and attachment. They seek relationships but fail to find satisfaction either in themselves or with others; it is almost as though there is a great contradiction between personal self-expression and growth, on the one hand, and interaction with another person in a relationship, on the other. What are these women really seeking in their endless struggle for both freedom and relationship? Individuation/de-individuation, the ability or lack of ability to stand on one's own, gets confused with attachment/detachment, the ability or lack of ability to reach out to others. Individuation — or independence — and detachment are easily confused, as are attachment and de-individuation. And that confusion leads to the misperception that a person gains freedom only by avoiding commitment and closeness — that one must sacrifice this freedom when he or she commits to a relationship.[1]

Pandora: The Other First Lady

This oppositional view between individuation and attachment can be seen in the Greek myth about the first woman, Pandora, whose name means "all gifts." Zeus, the father of the gods, decides to make life difficult for the first men by withholding from them the knowledge of fire. When Prometheus steals fire for man, Zeus responds by sending Pandora as a punishment.

It is important to understand the meaning of fire for primitive man to grasp how enslaving Zeus's actions are. Primitive humans are dominated by nature. Day and night are different worlds: by day, the light of the sun provides humans with a view of their surroundings. They can distinguish land from water, friendly animals from predatory ones, and the harmless snakes from the poisonous; the sun's heat offers relief from the cold. At night there is no sun to provide light or heat, and un-

1. Kalman J. Kaplan, *TILT: Teaching Individuals to Live Together* (Philadelphia: Brunner/Mazel, 1998).

friendly animals come out to feed. But fire changes all that: it generates light and heat to hold the environment at bay, and it provides the basis for technological advance and autonomy. By withholding fire, Zeus deprives man of this autonomy and keeps him subservient.

However, Prometheus, a Titan and Zeus's uncle, steals fire from Mount Olympus, the home of the gods. He hides it in a hollow fennel stalk and gives it to humans, enabling them to survive and to progress technologically. Zeus is furious when he learns what Prometheus has done, and he contrives a nasty trick to get his revenge. He calls on various gods and demigods to contribute to the making of a new creature. One gives this new creature a beautiful form and appearance; another gives her grace; still others give her useful skills such as weaving. But the sly god Hermes gives her terrible morals. Zeus is intensely pleased with the mischief he is about to wreak and laughs gleefully. This is Pandora, and he sends this beautiful but unpleasant creature to Epimetheus, the naïve brother of the wise Prometheus. Taken by Pandora's beauty, Epimetheus ignores his brother's warning never to accept any gift from Zeus.

One day the irresponsible Pandora decides to open the box that Zeus has sent along with her — a box filled with evils. And as soon as she opens it, all the evils fly out. She closes the lid as quickly as she can, but it's too late. Only one thing remains trapped in the box — hope. According to this myth, all the evils in the world today are there because they were released by this first *woman*. But even worse news is that Pandora has managed to hold hope in the box, and it alone remains unavailable to humans. Woman is the villain in this myth, and Zeus has given her to humankind not as a precious gift but as revenge. She is sly, dishonest, and secretive, and her immature inability to control her curiosity brings endless anguish to mankind. Only a fool, such as Epimetheus, would be deceived and trapped by her beauty. As a role model, Pandora offers an unpromising start for the history of Greek women.

In this narrative, Prometheus's gift of fire has given humans some autonomy, but Zeus's gift of the beautiful Pandora has kept man miserable and subservient. Or, to put it more broadly, though fire has brought the world of humans independence, the relationship with a woman has brought man the antithesis of independence. The only possibility for independence is for man to reject Pandora and any gift of the vengeful gods. Therefore, relationships with women are not the "tender trap" of the Frank Sinatra song but a sinister and dangerous entrapment. A woman does not simply domesticate a man; she brings about his ruin, stripping him of any autonomy he might have achieved.

This view finds expression in a number of myths about mother goddesses from other cultures of the ancient Middle East. The main elements of the stories involve a powerful goddess who falls in love with a mortal man, who then disappoints or betrays her in some way. Overwhelmed with guilt and unable to face the displeasure of the goddess, the man castrates himself — sometimes even kills himself. Such a goddess, Magna Mater, was brought to Rome in 204 B.C.E. as the Romans sought her help in winning the great war against Carthage. Worship of her later spread widely throughout the Roman Empire.

Highly visible in this and similar cults were the castrated priests — men dressed in women's clothes — who paraded, leaping and dancing to noisy music, through the streets of the empire's cities. They typically slashed themselves with knives and swords until blood flowed copiously. Spectators watching these processions were often so caught up in the intensity of the ritual that they, too, would bloody themselves, or even castrate themselves. Such cults have been found in other periods of history, such as the Valerians in early Christianity, the flagellants of medieval Europe, and the Skoptje in eighteenth-century Russia.

In the ancient myths of the Middle East that were concurrent with the narrative of Hebrew Scripture, goddesses seem to prefer castrated men. Perhaps it is because they are more docile and easier to control; or perhaps the goddess's demands are a supreme test of her male followers' loyalty and devotion. Apparently, men with strong, whole bodies cannot be trusted. The goddess must assert her power and control over them: they become her playthings, her "boy toys," and she can discard them when they no longer interest her.

When the woman is seen as a castrater of man, a sexual relationship is portrayed as a sinister rather than tender trap — and the origin of man's undoing. This is also the pattern of the Olympian story of creation. Gaea, the earth goddess, colludes with her son, Chronus, to castrate her husband and his father, Uranus, the sky god, as Uranus approaches her for intercourse. No wonder Greek men feared female sexuality! Woman is dangerous, and man runs the risk of losing his manhood in a sexual relationship with her. This fear of female sexuality contributed to the encouragement of the Greek male's interest in young boys. Indeed, one of the few acceptable female figures in classical Greece was Athena, the virgin goddess. Born from Zeus's head, she carried her *aegis* (shield) topped with a Medusa head, and she appeared to be removed from this dangerous female sexuality.

Yet what is man to do? Being alone is no solution either. While the Greek poet Hesiod's Pandora myth says that "Zeus has made women to be an evil to mortal men, with a nature to do evil," it also says: "Zeus gives man a second evil to pay for the good they had. Whoever avoids marriage and the sorrows that women cause, and will not wed, [that man] reaches deadly old age without anyone to tend his years."[2] It is clear that Zeus has no desire to help humans; nor does Prometheus's gift fully answer man's needs (indeed, it may well have been motivated as much by his conflict with Zeus as by his regard for mankind).

Greek literature in general portrays woman as, at best, a necessary evil. In Euripides' tragedy *Medea*, Jason, the protagonist, laments that "it would be better for children to have come into this world by some other means and women never to have existed. Then life would be good." It is striking that his wife, Medea, shares this debased view of women: "It would be better to serve in battle three times than bear one child." Medea's words are also reflected in the *maenads* (frenzied women) of Greek mythology. Described by Euripides in *The Bacchae*, as well as in other sources, *maenads* were ordinary women who would leave their homes for orgiastic dancing in the forests. There they would run around bare-breasted and suckle animal cubs; and they would tear animals apart and eat them raw.

2. Hesiod, *Theogony*, ll. 600-610.

In *The Bacchae,* the *maenads* are devotees of Dionysus, whom they adore as groupies do a rock star. King Pentheus of Thebes attempts to imprison Dionysus. When he is unsuccessful at that, he is finally persuaded to hide behind a tree to watch the *maenads,* including his own mother, Agave. The magic of Dionysus splits the tree and reveals Pentheus's presence. The *maenads* then tear Pentheus apart, and Agave herself carries her son's head into the city to her father Cadmus, believing it to be the head of a lion cub.

One of the disturbing things about this myth — among others! — is that the *maenads* find their freedom of expression only in these uncivilized and orgiastic activities that occur outside the confines of their family lives. It is as though they live subdued and submissive lives within their families and can find a sense of freedom only outside of them, even though this so-called freedom takes a destructive form. This is also the case with Pandora, who is never portrayed as having much of a personality herself. She is simply Zeus's plaything, sent to the world for the specific purpose of bringing trouble to mankind. As such, she is defined completely in terms of her relationship with men. Her character does not develop, and she removes the lid of the box in an act of malicious foolishness.

The fictional heroines of Western literature with whom we began this book seem to reflect these pessimistic ideas of classical Greece in their inability to integrate individuation and attachment. In *The Glory of Hera: Greek Mythology and the Greek Family,* sociologist Philip Slater points to the pathological nature of the Greek family in this regard, specifically with regard to male-female relationships — as well as parent-child relations — and tellingly observes that these tendencies have permeated contemporary Western society. Indeed, Slater states bluntly that "buried beneath every Western man is a Greek."[3] Bennett Simon extends Slater's argument in *Mind and Madness in Ancient Greece: The Classical Roots of Modern Psychiatry,* and he points to the dependence of modern psychiatry on these ancient Greek ideas,

3. Philip Slater, *The Glory of Hera: Greek Mythology and the Greek Family* (Boston: Beacon Press, 1968), p. 451.

9

suggesting that "the schizophrenic is terrified of both closeness and excessive distance."[4]

The idea that caring both for the self and for the other is internally contradictory has led people and cultures to cycle between these two unsatisfactory alternatives. For example, Simon compares Homer's two great epics in this regard, suggesting that "the *Odyssey* focuses far more than the *Iliad* on what it is to be in danger of isolation from one's own group."[5] Yosef Yerushalmi, in *Freud's Moses: Judaism, Terminable and Interminable,* argues that Freud carried this Greek cyclical view of history and sense of hopelessness into psychoanalysis and, we would add, into modern culture.[6]

From our perspective, the view of the self and the other as contradictory has led to emotional imbalances and ineffective solutions. One such solution involves prescribing that a person do the opposite of what he or she has been doing. Thus, selfishness is only resolved though merger with others, no matter how unhealthy that merger might be. Conversely, dependence is only resolved through isolation. In both cases, the antidotes are as polarizing as the initial problem. Alternatively, a compromise solution may involve trying to achieve a mathematical balance between self and other. None of this goes to the root of the problem.

Eve: The Helpmeet-Opposite

In contrast to Greek mythology, the God of Genesis introduces Adam to Eve and gives them both his blessing. The Hebrew Bible's view of woman's nature and her relationships with men is very different. Eve is created as a blessing and a "helpmeet-opposite" to Adam. But she is not defined solely in terms of her relationship to Adam; she is a per-

4. Bennett Simon, *Mind and Madness in Ancient Greece: The Classical Roots of Modern Psychiatry* (Ithaca, NY: Cornell University Press, 1978), p. 41.

5. Simon, *Mind and Madness,* p. 65.

6. Yosef H. Yerushalmi, *Freud's Moses: Judaism, Terminable and Interminable* (New Haven: Yale University Press, 1991), p. 95.

sonality with her own role in the divine plan. It is this independence that enables her to find freedom within her relationship with Adam — not in withdrawing from the relationship or destroying it.

The term "helpmeet" has lost some of its original meaning with the evolution of the English language (and has even degenerated into "helpmate" in popular parlance). In fact, it was two separate words and became one word (through popular usage) long after the King James Version of the Genesis 2:18 account of God's motivation for creating woman: "It is not good for the man to be alone; I will make an help meet for him" (Gen. 2:18). To the scholars who produced this great translation of the Bible in the early seventeenth century, "help meet" (two words) meant a "helper suitable" or a "fit support" for Adam. ("Meet," an adjective, was the now-archaic word for "fit" or "proper.") The space between the words was elided over time, and the phrase became misunderstood to be one word: "helpmeet." Referring to the woman in Genesis 2 as "helpmeet" portrays her as a suitable and equal companion for the man.

Yet, while this is certainly a positive portrayal of woman, the term "helpmeet" still falls short of the original Hebrew term *ezer kenegdo*. Literally and simply, this term means "helpmeet-opposite." The ancient midrash sees *ezer kenegdo* as embodying two parts: the woman in her relationship with a man is a supportive helper *(ezer)*, but when he is wrong, her support takes the form of opposing him *(kenegdo)*. At her best, the woman will be kind and supportive but also wise and independent — so as to set the man straight when he needs it. To be effectively *kenegdo* is a high form of kindness. Two very ancient Aramaic translations of Genesis interpret *ezer kenegdo* along these same lines: "corresponding support," which implies that a successful support must be a full partner, one whose strength and independence are comparable to and complement her mate's. The woman, like the man, is created in the image of God, and only thus can they carry on a healthy relationship in which both can grow.

Furthermore, the Bible does not portray Eve's entrance into the world as an attempt to strip man of his autonomy, as Pandora's entrance is portrayed in the Greek myth. The biblical account of creation as interpreted by the ancient Talmudic sages does not portray God as withholding fire from human beings. In fact, God provides the means for Adam to invent fire because God has compassion for him.[7] Nor is Eve sent as a punishment or a curse.

Eve is tempted by the serpent to eat of the fruit of the Tree of the Knowledge of Good and Evil with the promise that she will be like God, knowing good and evil (Gen. 3:5). The serpent's words prove false: its claim that a fruit contains "wisdom" is closer to the magical thinking of ancient paganism than it is to the biblical spirit of learning and knowing. Eve may not have fully comprehended that she and Adam were already knowledgeable and had freedom of choice. She is mistaken in her judgment, but she (and womankind in general) is not portrayed as a curse and the enemy of Adam's autonomy. Critical to a comparison of the stories of Pandora and Eve is the timing of woman's entrance into the world and the reasons she is created. Zeus sends Pandora to man *after* the human has obtained fire — as a trick and a punishment to take away his autonomy. He sends her not to help man but to bring him down. God sends Eve to Adam *before* the human act of eating of the fruit to be man's full partner, and to remain as his helpmeet-opposite.

There are times when the woman best fulfills her mission by agreeing with the man in her life and other times by opposing him; but both approaches can be positive and supportive. Sometimes this can mean acting together, and sometimes it means acting on one's own to make the decisions that require clear thinking and courageous dedication. The helpmeet-opposite knows how to handle crises well and to do what is needed to fulfill humanity's covenantal alliance with God.

A helpmeet-opposite interacts with a man in a relationship in such a way that the whole is more than merely the sum of two parts. There is no doubt that the people in a good partnership can do far more and far better together than the same two can do when each one acts separately. This is true at the level of working or intellectual partnerships; but it is even more true in expressing and fulfilling the human need to

7. Midrash Genesis Rabbah, 11:2.

love: as one discovers the dynamic of the other, one learns to be more free of anxiety about the self. One turns away from an overwhelming and debilitating sense of life's sadness and tragedy to a means of overcoming spiritual incompleteness.

Both the ancient literature of the Greeks and the Hebrew Midrash tell us that, at the very beginning of the world, the man and woman were actually one creature, not two. However, the details and meanings of the two versions of that human creation narrative differ starkly after that. In Genesis, God separates the man and the woman and then brings them back together in marriage as an act of kindness to Adam — so that "the man should not be alone." Why didn't God simply create separate males and females from the start, as he did with all the birds and beasts? The Midrash appears to suggest that a human being needs a special companion, such that the two people stay loyal and close to each other, providing each other an intimacy and trust that more occasional relationships cannot offer. Most animals do not need this kind of attachment: they mate with new partners whenever the time is right or the opportunity arises. Human beings find such irregular matings unsatisfying because each human relationship is unique.

In Plato's *Symposium,* Aristophanes tells a similar story of how the earliest people were made up of three sexes: men, women, and hermaphrodite circle people — a combination of the first two. These primeval hermaphroditic people were so mighty and arrogant that they even thought to ascend Mount Olympus and attack the gods. Consequently, Zeus decided to slice them in two — not to provide them with companions, as in the biblical account, but to humble their pride and weaken them, and thus make them more pliable to the gods. So the primeval people were indeed cut in half, and the longing to heal this division still brings people together today. Men may now yearn for women or men; women, too, may yearn for either sex, depending on what they consisted of before Zeus separated them. The desire that people feel toward each other expresses their ancient need to be reunited, not simply the desire for sexual activity. All of this is a result of mankind's wickedness and hubris, and if humans do not mend their ways, the myth goes, it is possible that Zeus will split them in half again.

Here the Greeks portray people, as they so often do, as finding little favor with the gods. But people seek a union with other people to accomplish a reattachment of something that was sundered. In quite stark contrast, the biblical view portrays God as a helpful and supporting parent who gives his blessing to a dynamic working union between two strong and united individuals, from which they can then work together in the pattern of the helpmeet-opposite. In this context, the Hebrew Bible gives women a radically new role and new importance in human history, just as it does the man. First, the helpmeet-opposite supports the man in harnessing the powerful instinct of the sexual drive. Within a sanctified marriage relationship, that drive can be redeemed and purged of its primitive and fearsome power and channeled into something productive and sacred — part of the intimacy, support, and interdependence of a couple. A couple is no longer merely generic male and female, denoting objects of gratification, but they are a man and a woman whose need to love is not essentially narcissistic but an expression of a drive that reaches out to give and receive love and to participate in God's mission.

Once again, the Hebrew *ezer kenegdo,* the helpmeet-opposite, will oppose her husband when he is wrong; indeed, she *must* oppose him in such a circumstance, but she must do this in a helpful rather than hurtful way, as his friend and not as his enemy. This difference extends to the role of women outside marriage and family as well. A helpmeet-opposite will express her opinions in the context of any relationship, whether at work, school, in the arts, athletics, or politics. A woman with a sense of being a helpmeet-opposite will not behave as do the unhappy heroines of Western literature we have observed above. She will be able to express her own unique personality and insight in her special voice. However, this creative self-expression is not to be confused with strident obstinacy for its own sake, which damages the larger context within which the woman is trying to operate, and leaves her, in fact, unable to express her own voice.

True and False Freedom

One weakness in contemporary Western society is its tendency to see the needs for individuation and attachment as incompatible: individuation is confused with detachment, and attachment with de-individuation. To be close to someone seems to impede personal freedom: in this thinking, one must be detached in order to be free — and enslaved in order to be attached. This leads to a false definition of freedom as isolation; it also leads to a false definition of intimacy or commitment as giving up one's freedom.

Individuation expresses real freedom: it is a person's ability and need to be mature, responsible, and independent, as well as to make suitable moral decisions. Detachment does not denote being able to act independently; rather, it is the inability to interact with others. A detached person is afraid of close relationships with others. Attachment and de-individuation are quite different as well. An attached person is one who is not afraid to extend his or her hand, one who enjoys being part of a family or community. This kind of person feels that needing people makes him or her, as in the Barbra Streisand song, "the luckiest people in the world." A de-individuated person, in contrast, is afraid of being free — or unable to be free — and looks to others in an attempt to compensate for his or her lack of independence. Consider the following clinical example of a young woman.

> Barbara, 28, came to marriage therapy focusing on a lack of direction in her life. Her complaint that she did not know "where she was going or who she really was" did not seem in character with her behavior with her husband. On the surface Barbara seemed affectionate and eager to spend time with her husband. As therapy progressed, however, it became clear that Barbara manifested an infantile clinging: seemingly trivial separations became the occasion for panic responses. The initial impression that Barbara was affectionate (that is, attached) was replaced by a sense that Barbara did not know who she was (that is, lack of individuation).

Likewise, "apartness" is open to several interpretations. Does one seek solitude to come to know oneself (individuation) or because of a fear of being involved with others (detachment)? Consider a second clinical example:

> Karen, 23, entered individual treatment complaining that she did not have close friends. This seemed to be a strange complaint because Karen was always surrounded by people — both male and female — and immersed in activities. However, in the course of therapy it became clear that she organized her schedule so as to minimize the possibilities of intimate contacts. In fact, she often went to desperate lengths to avoid one-on-one encounters. A superficial glance suggested that Karen was individuated; but closer examination revealed a fundamental fear of attachment.

The idea that caring for both one's self and the other is contradictory has led to a great deal of confusion. A solution often suggested is that a person do the opposite of what he or she is doing: thus one resolves selfishness only by merging with others, no matter how unhealthy. Conversely, it is often suggested that dependence can only be resolved via isolation. Both of these responses are as polarizing as the initial problem. Alternatively, a compromise solution may involve trying to achieve a mathematical balance between the self and the other. None of these goes to the root of the problem.

Consider an example that we have discussed in a companion book.[8] Lisa is a young physician who has been dating Rob. It is September and Rob's birthday is coming up, but Lisa is very busy. So Lisa sends her secretary out to get a new tie for Rob; the whole process takes no more than thirty minutes. When Lisa gives the tie to Rob, he thanks her, but his disappointment is tangible. He was expecting something more personal. Lisa feels guilty that she let Rob down, and she resolves to behave differently the next time.

8. Kaplan and Schwartz, *The Seven Habits of the Good Life* (Lanham, MD: Rowman and Littlefield Publishers, 2006), pp. 4-5, 110-13.

So now it is Christmas time, and Lisa is determined not to repeat her mistake. She sets aside an entire week to look for a present for Rob. She knows that he likes cameras, so she shops in one store after another in search of the perfect camera for Rob. When she finally chooses one, she presents it to Rob — and he is very happy. Lisa, however, does not feel so happy. She feels resentful that she has spent close to a week of what could have been productive time looking for something in which she doesn't really have a personal stake. And Lisa takes it out on Rob — in a variety of ways. She shows up late for scheduled dates with him, and she generally withholds emotion and intimacy from him.

When Rob's next birthday arrives, Lisa is in a quandary. She has concluded that having her secretary take thirty minutes to get a gift was too little involvement (leaving her feeling guilty), and forty hours was too much (leaving her feeling the martyr). So she decides to split the difference. Her halfway solution is to shop for twenty hours for a present for Rob — not too much (forty hours) and not too little (thirty minutes). Keeping her time limit in mind, she shops for a sweater that she thinks Rob will like. And she buys a sweater that is kind of nice, and Rob kind of likes it. Rob is a bit lukewarm about the gift, and Lisa in turn feels lukewarm about her efforts. She does not feel too guilty and on the other hand does not feel too martyred. Lisa doesn't feel put upon, and Rob doesn't feel neglected; but neither one feels that special either.

This is obviously not an ideal solution to the dilemma of the self and the other. Yet this halfway solution is exactly what many contemporary therapists have recommended. The family therapist Salvatore Minuchin (1974) describes the points of interchange between one member of a family and another. One kind of family is enmeshed or overinvolved: this family has diffuse boundaries, which results in a difficulty providing sufficient privacy. A disengaged or underinvolved family, in contrast, is described as having rigid boundaries. This kind of family will have difficulty promoting sufficient communication or intimacy. Minuchin sees healthy families as having clear boundaries, in the middle between diffuse boundaries and rigid boundaries. These families should allow for both some privacy and also some communication and intimacy. One should love, but one should not love too much: not loving enough means the loss of the other, but loving too much means a loss of one's self. A compromise would look something like the one represented by Lisa's solution of shopping for twenty hours rather than forty hours or thirty minutes.

This compromise is not really satisfactory. But what is wrong with it? Simply put, the love of self is not contradictory to love of the other. Lisa is not really doing what she wants with her time, and Rob is not really getting what he wants. So the question becomes twofold: What does Lisa want to do with her time? What does Rob want as a gift? As opposed to her feeling of merely going through the motions when she is doing things she doesn't want to do, Lisa enjoys her life and feels fulfilled when she spends her time doing what she likes to do. But what kind of time is that? It is self-expressive time. It is time when Lisa expresses something about herself, whether it involves achieving her professional goals in medicine, performing in athletics, writing, singing, building a table, cooking, composing a poem, or, indeed, giving a gift. For Lisa, it may involve something to do with her songwriting ability. If she can use her time developing and expressing this gift, she will not feel that it's a waste, but that it is expressive time well spent. Furthermore, if she can give a gift to Rob that is expressive of her inner being and her life purpose, she will not feel the opposition between self and other. She will experience the time she spends on writing a song for Rob as self-expressive. The more time she spends expressing herself to Rob, the better she will feel. And she doesn't need to limit the time she spends this way, because it is "alive time" — that is, time when she feels most alive. Why? Because Lisa's giving to Rob involves expressing and strengthening her own personality as well as pleasing him. Thus, Lisa is never more herself than when she expresses her love for Rob.

Now, what about Rob? He will value a gift that expresses care on the part of Lisa. If Lisa gives Rob a song that she has written specifically and expressly for him, he is quite likely to be very touched. Rob will likely feel that Lisa cares enough to really give of herself to him. The opposition of the self and the other — and the implicit struggle over time — is broken. Lisa's sense of self is not depleted by her love for Rob, and his receiving of her gift strengthens his sense of self.

This resolution does not represent an equivocating moderation that is simply designed to avoid extremes; instead, it is a full wholeness that redefines the entire situation. The couple can achieve a harmony that is wholehearted and full, balanced and not polarized, and not moderate in the sense of being only partially committed. One does not have to hold back to be balanced. The more developed the individual, the more fully she or he is capable of loving. Indeed, this is the biblical view of relationships and of the idea of a "helpmeet-opposite." Lisa has a sense of purpose in her life and is thus able to express her own individual self in her gift to Rob.

The helpmeet-opposite concept expresses itself in people working together, whether the need of the moment is to agree or to challenge the other. At its best, marriage is not a bitter rivalry but a mutual action of partners from which the partnership can draw great benefit. Biblically oriented partners understand that God is the third partner in the relationship. The helpmeet-opposite seeks to grow by interacting, and she does not need control: she understands that God is the ultimate guarantor of her life's work, including her relationship with her husband and with history. She can thrive whether working alone or with others, while the person (or nation) that does not see God as guarantor can fail, whether through isolation or enmeshment.

CHAPTER 2

The Biblical Model

This biblical model of woman seems far from what is extolled in modern society. What do men in Western societies want from women, and what do women want from themselves? Neither seems to know. The plethora of self-help books and online and off-line dating services indicates that people seem obsessed with finding the right partner. Yet, at the same time, many people in relationships seem to be looking for ways to get out of them. This repeats the classical Greek pattern and is reflected in the unhappy lives of the heroines of Western literature observed above.

The women of the Hebrew Bible (Old Testament) are radically different. Strong, wise, and independent, they have relationships with men that can be productive and mutually supportive. Most significantly, they have a deep sense of purpose and a powerful commitment to God's plan for the world in which they know they play a major part. Their intelligence and moral character — indeed, even their beauty — can all become part of their life's work. Strong in both spiritual and physical endeavors, these women are never subservient; they relate well to other people — both supporting others and being supported by them. Their value as human beings is known, and they deserve the recognition and praise they receive: "Give her of the fruit of her hands, and let her works praise her in the gates"

(Prov. 31:31). It is the very essence of their strength that they recognize the importance of what they do. These women acknowledge that all people are made in the image of God and that it is a person's duty and privilege to understand how important this is and to act accordingly.

Developing such an awareness requires a transformation in modern psychology to incorporate this biblical worldview within the concept of normal human development. Over fifty years ago Dr. Erich Wellisch, medical director of Grayford Child Guidance Clinic in England, called for a biblical psychology. This is what he said:

> The very word "psyche" is Greek. The central psychoanalytic concept of the formation of character and neurosis is shaped after the Greek Oedipus myth. It is undoubtedly true that the Greek thinkers possessed an understanding of the human mind which, in some respects, is unsurpassed to the present day, and that the trilogy of Sophocles still presents us with the most challenging problems. But stirring as these problems are, they were not solved in the tragedy of Oedipus. In ancient Greek philosophy, only a heroic fight for the solution but no real solution is possible. Ancient Greek philosophy has not the vision of salvation.
>
> No positive use has been made, so far, of the leading ideas of Biblical belief in the attempts of modern psychology to formulate basic findings and theories. But there is no reason why the Bible should not prove at least [as fruitful] if not more fruitful than the concepts of Greek or Eastern religious experience. . . . Psychology and theology are at the crossroads. The atheistic and pantheistic aspects of modern psychology lead to dangerous conclusions. The non-biological aspect of theology is doomed to lead to frustration. . . . There is need for a Biblical psychology.[1]

1. Erich Wellisch, *Isaac and Oedipus: Studies in Biblical Psychology of the Sacrifice of Isaac* (London: Routledge and Kegan Paul, 1954), p. 115.

Let's discuss the role of biblical women in more detail with respect to their roles as wives, daughters, mothers, and human beings in the world.

Women as Wives

Woman entered the Greek world as a curse to men, and, in a certain sense, she never overcame that difficult beginning. Woman became the mechanism of man's enslavement, and man had to avoid attachment to her to have any hope of freedom. But man does have sexual needs, and Pandora is irresistible: her sexuality and man's sexual desire combine to entrap him. Yet, though he must try to stay away from the woman in order to be free, it is not good for man to grow old alone. He seems to be forced into a perpetual choosing between freedom and attachment.

One solution that has emerged in Western society is to differentiate the whore and the virgin. Thus a man must desexualize his wife and redirect his sexual desires toward loose women outside the marriage — prostitutes, strippers, barmaids, and the like. Another defense involves vulgarizing sexual relations into a mechanical act: using expressions such as "screw" or "bang." This stratagem may temporarily alleviate man's dilemma, allowing him to fulfill his sexual needs while avoiding emotional attachment by converting the woman into a sexual object with no ability to entrap him. Yet this pattern can hardly be satisfactory in the long run. Male-female relationships of this kind are distant and devoid of the intimacy that human beings require. The physical act of sex becomes disconnected from love, and a man continues to avoid a genuine attachment to a woman because he fears it will limit his freedom.

Genesis's account of the creation of humans is very different. A benevolent and all-wise God creates humans as the culmination of six days of creation. The entire world has been prepared and made ready for them. Finally, late on the sixth day, God is ready: "Let us make man." He gathers dust from the earth to make the body and then breathes into him his own breath of life. God's first words to the people constitute a command and a blessing together: "Be fruitful and multiply and fill the earth. . . ." God does not create humans to lighten his workload or to be his messenger in a nasty trick. Genesis 2 tells us that God teaches Adam all about the plants and animals, and that Adam, with the vast knowledge he has learned from the divine scientist, classifies and gives names to all the animals. God shares with humans something very special to him: the gift of creativity and independence of thought and action, including even the power to act against God's wishes. No parent ever gave an adolescent child the keys to the family car with less reluctance.

Yet with all his early achievement, Adam is very alone and unfulfilled. God puts Adam into a deep sleep and separates part of his body, thus dividing the original human into two beings — a man and a woman. This is the creation of Eve as a helpmeet-opposite to Adam: rather than being a curse, she is an integral part of a complete human relationship. As noted above, biblical people were never designed to be mere automatons, or puppets of God, as were the first people in so many of the pagan myths. Nor were women designed only in terms of their relationship to men; Eve has her own place in God's plan for the world.

Eve is misled into seeing God's prohibition to eat of the Tree of Knowledge as an attempt to limit her and Adam rather than to ensure that they use their abilities to carry out their roles in God's creation. As a true helpmeet-opposite, Eve gives Adam the forbidden fruit, too, trying to help him free himself from what they have been misled into believing is subjugation. After they eat of the Tree of the Knowledge of Good and Evil, Adam and Eve do not suddenly gain in wisdom. Rather, they become uncomfortable with their nakedness: not about the fact that they are not wearing clothing, which they certainly know; rather, they feel unprotected and vulnerable. They make themselves garments of fig leaves, but they still call themselves naked, despite being well covered. Eve is mistaken in her judgment, like any of us can be. Eve's purpose is not to punish Adam but to help him, and Adam has nothing to fear from her or from her sexuality. Adam should not have blamed Eve for giving him the forbidden fruit, because it meant that he was ultimately blaming God for giving him Eve.

But what exactly are the consequences? Adam and Eve disobey God and find it difficult to deal with their disobedience. They are expelled from Eden, and they will no longer live indefinitely. They will have to struggle and work hard. Even after having done wrong, Eve does not wholly lose her cool. When confronted by God, she explains what happened in dignified, almost poetic language: "The serpent beguiled me." God still loves Eve, and his words to her are certainly not a curse (only the serpent was cursed, not the people) and not even so much a punishment as an attempt to help her define her situation. There shall now be pain for her in the bearing and raising of children, "and to your husband shall be your desire and he shall rule over you" (Gen. 3:16).

Although this statement is often seen as denoting punishment for Eve, we suggest a different reading. The aim of the first part of this statement to Eve is not to be punitive, to express divine pique, or to cause her unwarranted difficulty, but rather as a correction that is intended to guide Eve to carry on her unique creative work as the beloved creation of God. When David says to God in Psalm 23, "Your rod and your staff comfort me," he understands the divine application of the rod to a person as a benevolent correction toward a much higher purpose. David believes that the administration of God's rod to a person is a correction and guide from God as a benevolent shepherd.

The second part of the statement in Genesis 3:16 is not meant to give the man license to lord it over the woman as an inferior slave-partner or to cause her to lose her status as a helpmeet-opposite. What it does mean is that the woman seems to have some conflict over her drive to freedom: she confuses being independent (individuated) with being rebellious (detached). This is a problem that she must be aware of. In the eyes of God she remains free and indeed obligated to be moral, to develop her full human abilities and creativity and to learn to make right choices and decisions in her life. Like the man, she will find her fullest freedom and creativity through her service to God.

Although the two people are sent out of the Garden, their humanity and greatness remain intact, and they can still have significant lives. The woman is told that she will bear children in pain, but Adam also gives her a new name, Eve (Hebrew *havva*), which means "mother of life." Adam and Eve are now aware of their essential nakedness, but God signals his recognition and empathy in their new situation by giving them warm and pleasant garments to replace the unsightly fig leaves. Further, he provides for the continuation of human life through Seth, their third son, born years after Cain's murder of Abel.

Certainly, the biblical message in all this is far different from the message of the Greek myth. Attachment is not seen as inconsistent with freedom, nor is woman a block to man's autonomy. Sexual relations with a woman are not to be feared by the man. In the biblical view there is no stigma attached to the female, and sexual love is a blessing. When Genesis refers to Adam "knowing" Eve, it is both a physical and a spiritual knowing. The Bible's view is that the preferred state for any human is marriage. Yet the women in these biblical marriages are not mindless. All through the Bible there are women of remarkable intelligence and character, great personalities in their own right, who contribute much to the story of God and humanity. At the same time, they are significant figures within their families, supporting their husbands when the situation warrants it and opposing their husbands when that is the right course. They know that they have their own role in the divine plan (Gen. 2:18). The biblical woman is not portrayed as castrater and destroyer, but as nurturer.

The Greek and Hebrew terms for "womb" are strikingly different. The Greek term is *hystera,* from which English word "hysteria" is derived. The *hystera* is a source of labile and mercurial affect; woman, even in the Freudian scheme, is seen as unstable and as an unreliable source of morality. The biblical term for "womb" is *rehem,* which has quite a different connotation: it is connected to the Hebrew word *rahamim,* which means "mercy" or "compassion," a term of great praise that is used to describe God himself. In this view, woman is anything but unstable; she provides a secure base for human development.

Throughout the Hebrew Bible, women are typically portrayed as figures with great moral strength who express their humanity in areas of human relations and in service before God. Women like Sarah and Rebecca play major roles in carrying out the divine mission of building a new faith and nation based on monotheism, wisdom, and love. To carry out this mission, a woman may need to do many things, beginning with the support she gives as wife and mother and going on to the wide range of emotional, economic, and social activities attributed to the "woman of valor" in Proverbs 31. In Mark Twain's story "Adam's Diary," Adam says that he treasured Eve more and more as time went on, for he learned that, though they had been sent out of the garden, wherever she was, was Eden for him.

Fathers and Daughters

Let us now examine father-daughter relationships in Greek and biblical families. A father in Greek literature typically carries uncertain feelings about his own manhood into the relationship with his daughter and transmits ambivalent signals to her. He demands her adoration while, at the same time, he demeans her. If the daughter does not idealize him, the father threatens her with rejection and abandonment. She, in turn, feels that she deserves such treatment, as in the story of Agamemnon and Iphigenia. Iphigenia, like many young girls, suffers from low self-esteem, and she desperately wants her father's attention. She prefers him to her mother and is willing to be put to death to please her father, thinking it will bring her closer to him: "O mother, blame me not! Let me go first and put my arms about my father's neck."[2]

But Agamemnon focuses only on his own feelings and seems to have no empathy for his daughter or her predicament: "O *my* wretched fate!" (l. 1135; italics added). Iphigenia pleads with her father for life and recognition, revealing her feeling of powerlessness: "I have only tears. . . . They are all my power. I clasp your knees; I am

2. Euripides, *Iphigenia in Aulis*, ll. 631-35.

your suppliant now. I am your own child; my mother bore me to you. O kill me not untimely!" (ll. 1215-18). He ignores her pleas, and she cannot express her sense of betrayal and anger directly to him. She complains instead to her mother, Clytemnestra: "Mother, my father has gone, left me, betrayed and alone!" (ll. 1313-15). Iphigenia gives herself over to the total idealization of her father and, simultaneously, to utmost self-debasement by dying to preserve his honor. Perhaps she feels that accepting her fate with courage will ultimately win her father's approval.

Another Greek story of father and daughter involves Oedipus and Antigone. Antigone obsesses over the incestuous marriage of her parents: "Alas for the wretched mother's slumber at the side of her own son — and my sire! From what manner of parents did I take my miserable being!"[3] She sees this sin as a curse that will lead to her own death: "And to them I go thus, accursed, unwed, to share their home" (l. 869). Antigone seems obsessed with dying in order to fulfill her relationship with Oedipus (ll. 1-3). She even views death as a sort of marriage (ll. 808-14); furthermore, her death by hanging mimics that of her mother, Jocasta (ll. 1219-21). Perhaps this is Antigone's way of replacing Jocasta as Oedipus's wife — or even his mother.

Even more curious is Antigone's obsession with burying her dead brother in defiance of the order of her uncle, King Creon, a defiance interpreted by many scholars as the height of individualism. Nevertheless, she reveals a deep and unhealthy enmeshment with her family of origin when she declares that she would not have felt compelled to bury a husband or child as she would a brother: "The husband lost, another might have been found, and child from another to replace the first born: but father and mother hidden with Hades, no brother's life could bloom for me again" (ll. 909-13). This enmeshment is bad enough if we take Antigone's concern to be directed toward her slain brother, Polynices. We should remember, however, that her father, Oedipus, is also her brother! This desire to merge is clearly expressed in her wish to lie with her "brother" in death: "I shall rest, a loved one with him

---

3. Sophocles, *Antigone*, ll. 859-68.

whom I have loved" (l. 74). Although deeply enmeshed with her father, Antigone can nonetheless show cold indifference toward her lover, Haemon, and harsh antagonism toward King Creon.

Daughters in the Bible behave differently. They are entrusted with important responsibilities. It is the young but wise Miriam who is sent out by her parents to watch out for the safety of the little basket with her brother Moses in it as it floats on the Nile River (see chapter 3). This daughter does not idealize her father in the same desperate way, and the father sees the daughter as a real person whose advice and opinions are worthy of respect and attention, and not simply as a pawn to use in his war with his wife. The episode of the five daughters of Zelophehad (Numbers 27) supports this picture of benevolent and realistic father-daughter relations. After the death of their father, the unmarried daughters successfully approach Moses with the claim that, in the absence of brothers, they themselves should inherit the father's portion of the land so that his name should not be removed from his family (see chapter 5). The young women have a realistic view of their father: they neither idealize him nor reject him.

Mothers and Sons

There is a certain natural instinctive love of a mother toward a child. Yet this natural love can be altered or depleted, whether by individuals or by society as a whole. What happens when a child is sickly or irritable or in some way does not meet the mother's standard of what a child of hers should be? Not every social group has been welcoming toward new children, and many individuals are too selfish or unfeeling to care even about their own offspring. In Greek society, where we have already seen so much dysfunction (including child exposure and infanticide), it is not surprising to find that motherhood was not highly respected; indeed, mothers had little respect for *themselves*. Athena and Artemis, two of the major goddesses, remained virgins, and it is not clear whether Hera, the consort/sister of Zeus, ever had any children. How different this is from the biblical and traditional view of mothers, as well as the wise and loving grandmothers, that is very much a part of our American and ethnic cultures.

Greek literature includes many stories that depict mothers as showing little interest in sons. The occasions when they do seem to interact closely are when they become allies with their sons to destroy the father. This is the repeated pattern in the Olympian story of creation, described in Hesiod's *Theogony* (ll. 165-85). (The infant Zeus himself was saved from being swallowed by his father Cronus through a deception [ll. 455-90].) The abandoning and destructive side of the Greek mother is portrayed in Euripides' drama *Medea*. The heroine kills her two sons in an effort to hurt her husband, Jason, after she has already used them to deliver a poisoned gown to murder Jason's new wife. She shows no interest in raising children or building a family. When she is frustrated, she readily wishes for total destruction: "Let the whole house crash." When Medea hesitates, for just a moment, in her plan to murder the children, it is because she wonders who will take care of *her* in her old age and who will give her an honorable burial. She expresses no regret at the purposeless waste of young lives entrusted to her care.

It is clear that Medea is a deeply disturbed woman, but Euripides attributes her bad behavior not so much to herself as to the gods: "Many things the gods achieve beyond our judgment. What we thought is not confirmed and what we thought not god contrives." All of Medea's misery, both what she suffers and what she causes, is the gods' doing. In such a view of the world, children are simply an added burden. As the plot develops, Medea expresses her misery at being a woman and her resentment toward both Jason and her sons: "Curse you and your father too, ye children, damned sons of a doomed woman! Ruin seize the whole family!" (ll. 112-14). And both she and Jason demean the woman's role: "And yet they say we live secure at home, while they are at the wars, with their sorry reasoning, for I would gladly take my stand in battle array three times o'er, than once give birth" (ll. 244-51).

In Jason's view, men are truly superior, and women bring ruin: "Yea, men should have begotten children from some other source, no female race existing; thus would no evil ever have fallen on mankind" (ll. 573-75). Medea resents Jason's disdain for her sex, but she basically agrees with him: she is disgusted with being a woman and a mother herself. Her solution is horrible, not only frighteningly inhuman to others but self-destructive as well. Jason may now hate her, but he can no longer ignore her as weak, powerless, and irrational; she has proven herself to be more clever, more macho, and more destructive than any warrior (ll. 1370-1406). She punishes Jason for abandoning her and, at the same time, repays her sons for making her a mother and contributing to her abasement. Medea does not acknowledge her sons as individuals with their own right to live, but sees them simply as enmeshed extensions of herself.

The Bible's view of motherhood is in profound contrast to that of the women of Greek mythology. Going beyond mere maternal instinct, there is another factor that engenders great maternal love for a child: Genesis views humans as the culmination of God's creation, and women have a fundamental role in the trajectory of the divine plan for the world. At the end of six remarkable days, God formed the first human beings, and his first words to them were: "Be fruitful and multiply and fill the earth." God commanded and blessed those new humans with the ability to create. No other human act can equal the level of creativity and blessing that comes with bearing and raising another human being. Thus it is not surprising how many stories in the Bible are about women who are eager to bear children despite problems with infertility and other setbacks. Abraham and Sarah bring Isaac into the world when they are both advanced in age, and Rebecca and Rachel also have difficulties with fertility. The longing of these women for children is an important theme in Genesis. When they do have children, they see in their children a future that will be the fulfillment of a historic mission. The children are links in the chain that began with God's loving creation and continues on to a messianic age. They will grow up to fulfill God's work and purpose in the world. For the mothers of these children, life has deep meaning, which they are willing and happy to pass on to their children — because it is their highest calling.

The woman of the Hebrew Bible has no need to set her sons

against her husband in murderous rivalry, as the Greeks Gaea and Rhea did. She has very important things to do, and those things can best be done when there is harmony in the relationship between parents, children, and God. Indeed, the biblical woman will often act to strengthen a relationship between her husband and her sons. One might observe that Rebecca does act to prevent her husband Isaac from bestowing his blessing of material wealth and power on Esau because she wants it for Jacob; yet she still loves both sons, and she sends Jacob away to avoid violence between them (see chapter 7). The biblical narrative of Hannah and her son provides another example of a far-sighted and supportive mother (see chapter 7).

In strong contrast is Hagar's treatment of Ishmael in the desert. After the bread and water that Abraham has given them are gone, she casts the child under a shrub and goes some distance off, saying, "Let me not look upon the death of the child" (Gen. 21:16). She seems more concerned with her own feelings than her son's welfare (see chapter 8). This kind of selfish sensitivity is found among the Greeks, as when the goddess Artemis withdraws from the dying Hippolytus.[4] But it is not typical of a biblical mother, who, rather than forsaking her son, helps him in every way she can.

Mothers and Daughters

The basic relationship between mother and daughter in the Greek literary tradition is tainted by a lack of genuine self-esteem. Woman is seen as the mysterious "other," closely associated with the devouring earth, and Pandora is seen as a curse upon man. In his tragedy *Electra,* Euripides portrays Electra, the daughter of Agamemnon and sister of Iphigenia, to be waiting for years, completely obsessed by plans for the return of her brother, Orestes, and their revenge on their mother, Clytemnestra, for her murder of Agamemnon. We will discuss this story in more detail in the epilogue; at this point it is neces-

4. Euripides, *Hippolytus,* ll. 1432-33.

sary only to indicate that Electra feels debased as a woman: she not only hates herself, but is also hostile to both her mother and to men in general. After murdering her mother in revenge for the death of her father, Electra's major concern in life is that no one will now marry her (ll. 1198-1200).

A second mother-daughter narrative involves the relationship between Hecuba and her daughter Polyxena, which is described in Euripides' *Hecuba*. The widow of King Priam of Troy, Hecuba is a captive of the Greeks. Her first speech reveals the depths of her own despair and her distaste for life:

> Woe, woe is me! What champion have I? Sons, and city — where are they? Aged Priam is no more; no more my children now. Which way am I to go? . . . Ye have made an end, an utter end of me; life on earth has no more charm for me.[5]

When Hecuba learns that Polyxena will be sacrificed to the ghost of Achilles, her emotional structure crumbles so badly that she cannot function as a mother. Polyxena attempts to talk to her mother about her impending disaster, but Hecuba is unable to focus on anything but her own problems. When Polyxena says, "Unwedded I depart, never having tasted the married joys that were my due!" (l. 416), Hecuba replies: "Tell them of all women I am most miserable" (l. 424). And Hecuba transmits this fatalism to her daughter: "Alas, my daughter. Woe for thy life! . . . Ah, my daughter, a luckless mother's child" (ll. 179-85). Polyxena responds in kind:

> Alas, for thy cruel sufferings! My persecuted mother! Woe for thy life of grief! . . . No more shall I thy daughter share thy bondage, hapless youth on hapless age attending! . . . For thee I weep with plaintive wail, mother doomed to a life of sorrow! For my own life, its ruin and its outrage, never a tear I shed; nay, death is becoming to me a happier lot than life. (ll. 200-216)

5. Euripides, *Hecuba*, ll. 163-70.

The biblical view of mother-daughter relationships is in very stark contrast to this image. One of the Hebrew Bible's most noted exemplars of commitment along with independence is Ruth (see chapter 5). Naomi and her daughter-in-law Ruth maintain a loving and supportive relationship, which survives the death of not only Naomi's husband but her sons, one of whom is Ruth's husband. After her husband dies, and then both her sons die, Naomi urges her daughters-in-law, both widowed as she has been, to go off on their own; she says that she is too old to have any more sons for them to marry (Ruth 1:11-12). Naomi does not see her daughters-in-law simply as objects or as pawns in a cultural system; she sees them as people in their own right. But Ruth refuses to abandon Naomi:

> Entreat me not to leave you, or to return from following after you: for wherever you go, I will go; and wherever you lodge, I will lodge: your people shall be my people, and your God, my God. Where you die, will I die, and there will I be buried. The LORD do so to me, and more also, if anything but death parts you and me. (Ruth 1:16-17)

Unlike Clytemnestra, Naomi does not try to diminish Ruth's self-esteem in order to bind Ruth to her; she unselfishly urges Ruth to go her own way to find a husband. But when Ruth elects to remain with her mother-in-law and to return with her to Israel, an alien land to her, Naomi facilitates her marriage to her own kinsman Boaz. And when Ruth and Boaz have a son (her grandson), Naomi becomes the baby's nurse.

Women as Individual Humans

According to the book of Genesis, God separates the first woman from the original man. She is a beloved part of God's new world and the culmination, in a sense, of creation. Eve and Adam go through a difficult experience in the Garden of Eden, but Adam comes to understand better the singular qualities of this woman. After all that has happened, she has helped to fill his emptiness; and she has helped human beings come closer to God and to themselves. Unlike Pandora, Eve has brought growth and continuation to the world, not discord and destruction.

Women have a unique role as bearers and givers of life: their bodies are the source of new children and of nourishment for those children. And in the Bible, life *is* holiness. The absence of life makes the corpse ritually unclean because it is utterly diminished when life has left it. Perhaps it is women, more than men, who epitomize a sense of life organically and intuitively. Whereas a man can seek a breath of immortality largely through striving and achieving, a woman can attain immortality also in being a repository of humanity. She has an intimate feel for the flow of life — of birth and death. The Bible views a woman's ability to bear and raise children not as limiting her in any way, but as empowering her.

The book of Proverbs, part of that segment of Scripture known as "Wisdom Literature," contains many ideas and aphorisms relevant to women. Let us note three verses that describe women as teachers and providers of wisdom. The first praises the wisdom of one's mother: "Son . . . do not forsake the teaching of your mother" (1:8). The concept of "the teaching of your mother" can be understood on many levels, but the Scripture's use of this particular metaphor emphasizes the importance of the mother in the formation of a child's personality and later success. A second verse refers to wisdom as a sister: "Say to wisdom, 'You are my sister'" (7:4). One should feel as close and loving to wisdom and knowledge as one is toward a sister. The third verse distinguishes between a wise and foolish woman: "The wisest of women builds her house, but a fool tears it down with her own hands" (14:1). The wise woman understands that good things need to be worked on and strengthened, whether in material or spiritual needs. Her moral strength is essential in maintaining and building her "house."

The key to a woman's success is her faith in God and her understanding of how important her thoughts and actions are in God's plan for history. The biblical helpmeet-opposite can be peace-loving and supportive; but she can also fight when she needs to, because she understands the higher purposes of her existence. This woman also has unique ways of expressing her piety. She may be highly devout, constantly praying and talking to God, so that the bread she bakes and the clothes she wears are themselves an ongoing prayer. Her faith is very deeply rooted both in her love of God and her sense of the world around her.

It is noteworthy that the Bible often mentions the beauty of women — Sarah, Rebecca, Rachel, Esther, and others. Beauty can be an enhancement and is, in any case, part of a person's life. Yet the Bible is not voyeuristic, and the book of Proverbs will later opine that "charm is futile, and beauty is vain, but a woman who fears the Lord, she shall be praised" (31:30). Beauty and charm are blessings like any others, and they must be accepted and used as such in the service of the Creator. As part of what appears to be a wedding song for a king and his bride (45:1-13), the psalmist-poet offers insight and instructs the new queen that "all the glory of a king's daughter is within." Every woman has a certain glory, and she should be aware of it; yet the essence of that glory is inner — it is what she is herself. This does not mean that the woman should be sequestered in her house or limited in any way in developing her full humanity, which is in contrast to the Greco-Roman writer Plutarch's advice to young brides: Stay in your houses and accept your husband's teaching and guidance in all matters. This elevated status also creates responsibilities. The woman's work is essential to the development of the house and the character of the family members. The verse also appears to praise modesty, an inclination to avoid excessive showiness. A woman's real modesty is not to think of herself as less than she is, but it is to know who she is and to make use of her abilities, to be grateful to her Creator for blessing her, and to accept the responsibilities that make her truly human.

How different is the idea of woman's beauty in the literature of ancient Greece. Pandora is as troublesome and foolish as she is beautiful. Helen is the world's most beautiful woman, but she becomes ensnared by her own beauty: already married to Menelaus, she is forced by the goddess Aphrodite to run away with the Trojan prince Paris —

merely to fulfill Aphrodite's own promise to Paris to give him the world's most beautiful woman. Nor was woman's beauty necessarily prized by Greek men, who often sought beauty in young men or in statues rather than women. Many may have wished, as Jason did, that women had never existed and that men could have had children some other way.

This same wish is expressed in the myth of Deucalion and Pyrrha, who survive the great flood on an ark (though in the Greek account it is Prometheus, not Zeus, who provides the blueprint for the ark). After the waters recede and the couple leaves their ark, Deucalion throws stones over his shoulder and they become men, while Pyrrha throws stones over her shoulder and they become women — a recipe for reproductive cloning that is completely alien to the biblical concept of sexual union. Greek goddesses can be beautiful, and statues can reach toward perfection; but a woman's beauty is of less interest, hardly worth noting and hardly to be expected — or cherished — in a real-life human female. Greek myths could idealize beauty in cold statues, but Scripture sanctifies it in warm-blooded people. That Scripture itself praises the beauty as well as the character of its women makes it easier for biblical women to accept themselves physically, as well as spiritually, and to embrace the harmonious blending of the physical and spiritual.

Biblical women are simultaneously individuated and nurturing as they move toward their higher purpose. Greek heroines, in contrast, tend to be detached and/or enmeshed. Nor do they feel their part in the flow of history. The thinking of Greek women, with the exception of the virginal Athena, was typically disparaged and feared. The biblical woman can be very supportive as well as individualistic, beautiful as well as confident, and pious as well as strong. She is the helpmeet-opposite not only to her husband, but also to her children, to other people, and — in a sense — to God. She may enjoy jewels and may be enhanced by them, but diamonds are not the biblical woman's best friend. Her faith and her children are her jewels, and her best friends are her God, her family, her people, and her good life.

Let us now examine the stories of some of these women of the Bible.

CHAPTER 3

Love and Devotion

"A virtuous woman is a crown to her husband" (Prov. 12:4). And so it is with a woman who can genuinely love. Love is not simply sexual or material; yet it is not wholly spiritual either. Rebecca is drawn to Isaac for his character before she knows he is the son of her kinsman Abraham. Likewise, Isaac's servant Eliezer has noted Rebecca's kindness before he gets to know her family. Family connection is important, but only if the spiritual connection exists with it. Nor is love simply an outer display of emotion. Rizpah mourns in quiet dignity the deaths of her two sons, and she guards their bodies for many weeks in a way that greatly moves King David.

Bathsheba exemplifies yet a third aspect of a woman's love — the capacity to empathize with a man's inner being. Bathsheba may not be as politically astute as some others; yet she is a woman one can talk to and a woman who will try to help others. The story of Samson, Hazzelelponi, and Delilah only deepens this contrast. Delilah may have at one time loved Samson, but this does not keep her from using deception and her feminine wiles to betray him. Hazzelelponi, by contrast, shows the capacity to accept deeply and appreciate a man for what he is rather than what she wants him to become.

The Courtship of Rebecca (Genesis 24)

Abraham was growing older; his wife, Sarah, had already died, and it was time to find a wife for their son, Isaac. This was a most important matter, because Isaac would be the main continuer of the covenant God had made with Abraham, and also because Isaac was a very spiritual man who would need a woman who could appreciate him and his mission.

Scripture relates in detail that Abraham entrusted Eliezer, his steward, with the job of traveling to Haran and finding a bride among Abraham's family, who still lived there. Abraham is adamant that his son not take a wife from among "the daughters of the Canaanites, among whom I dwell." Eliezer must go to the land from which Abraham has come to find Isaac's future spouse among the households of Abraham's brothers. The Bible tells the story more or less from Eliezer's viewpoint. Let us here tell it more from Rebecca's angle; for as much as this is Eliezer's chapter, it is equally the story of Rebecca's wisdom, truthfulness, and kindness.

A comely young woman, Rebecca, comes out one evening to fill her pitcher with water at the public well. She does not stop to flirt with the young men, none of whom seems to know her well. Nor does she at first give much attention to a group of men with ten camels who appear to have just come in from a long journey. She goes down to the well, fills her pitcher, puts it on her shoulder, and is quickly on her way home when one of the travelers runs after her. "Let me please have a sip from your pitcher," he says (Gen. 24:17). Rebecca does not know who he is, but he is presumably thirsty and tired after his long journey. Rebecca is not a very loquacious young woman, so she responds briefly but respectfully, "Drink, sir," and she brings the pitcher down from her shoulder and gives it to him to drink from. For the moment, she gives him her full attention — until he is completely satisfied. Then she says, "I will draw water also for your camels until they have finished drinking." Again, with alacrity, Rebecca makes a number of trips down to the well, carrying up water to the trough until there is enough for all ten thirsty camels. The man is overwhelmed, for

Rebecca appears to be the answer to his prayers. "The man," as the text calls him, is Eliezer, Abraham's steward.

Eliezer might have inquired directly as to where Abraham's relatives were living, but he has come to this well first. He is on a very spiritual task and has sought only God's help and guidance. He has prayed to God: "Behold, I stand at the well, and the young women of the city go forth to draw water. Let it be that the young woman to whom I will say, 'Incline your pitcher and let me drink,' and if she will say 'Drink and I will give your camels to drink as well' — let her be the one you have seen as fit for your servant Isaac" (24:13-14). The qualities most needed in a woman who would join Abraham's family are kindness and hospitality: these are foundational concepts of Abraham's way of life. Eliezer now watches, dumbfounded, as Rebecca carries the water, amazed that God has answered his prayer so swiftly, for the young woman is not only generous and quick with her efforts on his behalf, but she is also physically beautiful and empathic with both people and animals. Eliezer can see that Rebecca is a young woman who will do someone a favor and who wishes to do kindness to others in general, who has the character, wisdom, and strength to give spontaneously and unstintingly of what she has and of herself.

The Midrash says that Eliezer saw another unique quality in this remarkable young woman: when she took the steps down to the well, "the water rose up to meet her." The Midrash speaks in many tones, and exactly what this passage means is difficult to ascertain; but it may suggest that Rebecca has achieved a certain wholeness and unity with God and his creation.

When the camels have finished drinking, the man asks Rebecca who her parents are. She answers in her usual informative and polite way that her parents are indeed part of Abraham's family. Eliezer then puts a golden ring on her nose and golden bracelets on her arms and bows in prayer, thanking God for having led him to the fulfillment of his trust (24:47-48). In addition to having a strong and generous character, the young woman comes from a good family. Since Rebecca is not materialistic or avaricious, it does not seem likely that she would accept Eliezer's gifts if she has not already perceived more or less who Eliezer is and why he has come to the well at Haran.

When Rebecca's family asks if she wishes to leave immediately to go to Canaan and her husband-to-be, her answer is again one simple and sufficient word — *elekh*, "I will go" (24:58). She is pleased with what has happened and glad to become the wife of Isaac and share in the founding of the new biblical faith. Rebecca sees a real future for herself with Isaac, with whom she can fulfill the wisdom and purpose of her character. She has met Eliezer and has loved his account of his vow with God; she has then heard Eliezer's prayer of thanks. Her own family can be generous and hospitable, but they are also rather acquisitive and can be idolaters. For example, when Rebecca comes home from the well with her gifts from Eliezer, her brother Laban becomes all excited — not about the possibility of his sister's marriage to Isaac, but about her new golden ornaments (24:30).

Rebecca accepts these and other gifts, but she sees far beyond them to a greater destiny for herself. Abraham's family is wealthy, but had Rebecca married Isaac only for his money, they would have had a miserable life together. Rebecca and several of her maidens now join Eliezer's caravan for the journey to Hebron and to Isaac. As the caravan proceeds along, one evening Rebecca raises her eyes and sees a man walking toward them. Isaac is walking in the field, perhaps to pray and meditate or simply to check his crops. Rebecca is a fine observer of human behavior, and she is struck by the man's genuine dignity. She alights from her camel so that she will not appear to be sitting over him and asks Eliezer who the man is. She is not accustomed to inquire about strange men, but she already realizes that this is no chance meeting. Isaac and Rebecca are married, and she is able to restore to Abraham and Isaac's household much of the light, blessing, and love that have been missed since Sarah's death.

FROM ALL SIDES, this story points to a rejection of a materialist way of selecting a mate. Eliezer does not set criteria of wealth or position; instead, he pledges himself to God. What matters to him is that the potential spouse for Isaac should show kindness — as exemplified by the way she acts toward him and his caravan. He hopes the woman will be in the family of Abraham; but he does not explicitly include this condition in his request. God does not reply in words, but the unfolding story reveals that Eliezer's mindset is in line with God's plan. Eliezer observes that Rebecca seems to be at one with what she is doing, and he proceeds to test his intuitions. He tells her that he is thirsty, and she responds most graciously by giving him what he has asked for — and with more than he has requested. Impressed with Rebecca's kindness, Eliezer decides that she is fit to be the wife of Isaac, making that decision even before knowing that she is of Abraham's family. But both of his considerations are essential elements of this story.

Rebecca continues to operate in her ingenuous way, accepting Eliezer's offer to marry Isaac without demanding extensive assurances about Isaac's material wealth and status. This pattern repeats itself in such a way that, when she arrives in Caanan, Rebecca is drawn to Isaac's genuine dignity before she even knows who he is. Isaac is delighted to learn that Rebecca is a kinswoman of his. This integration of the spiritual and the familial is not incidental or coincidental; finding a mate from a proper family is important but not sufficient. Eliezer has based his judgment on spiritual factors, but this does not mean that other realities can be ignored. That Rebecca is of Abraham's family makes it more likely that she and Isaac will have a common purpose.

Bithia (Exodus 2)

An animal that has sufficient food, shelter, and companionship, as well as a suitable mate in the proper season, will probably be very content. But a human being is different. Put a human in a situation in which he or she has all the food, companionship, sex, and entertainment that he or she can handle, and this person will become, after a time, very dissatisfied. This is because humans have an existential drive, a sense of wanting to be better and more than they are in both body and soul. Humans need a sense of purpose and the satisfaction of progressing toward fulfilling it. It is typically the loss or confusion of this existential purpose that causes people to suffer those periods of indecision and self-doubt that we call adolescent crises, midlife crises, and all the life-cycle crises. Developing and improving one's wisdom and sense of purpose at each stage of life is the best approach toward handling it successfully.

An Egyptian princess in that civilization's flourishing Empire Age was one of the wealthiest and most powerful women in the world, a royal personage living in the splendor and ease that immense power and wealth had produced. Yet the princess of this story does not find meaning in the glorious opulence of the royal palace. Instead, she experiences a need to give love and compassion and to gain a freedom that the empire does not offer. And thus she saves the life of a baby who will grow up to free his people from the cruelty of slavery in Egypt.

This man who led his people out of that bondage had a number of names. Yet Moses, the name given to him by the Egyptian princess, is the one always used in Scripture. This brief story in Exodus 2 never mentions the princess's name, but tradition identifies her as Bithia, the daughter of Pharaoh. Later, she will leave Egypt with the Israelites, will be with them in the Sinai, and still later will marry Caleb, a leader of the tribe of Judah.

As Exodus 1:22 recounts, Pharaoh has decreed that all newborn boys of the Israelites are to be thrown into the Nile. A Levite woman gives birth to a son, and she and her husband hide him for three months. Seeing that they can no longer keep him safe, the mother makes a little basket-boat and places the child in that makeshift boat in the reeds of the river, leaving his sister to watch him from a distance. Perhaps the mother is hoping that God will watch over her child and that a friendly hand will rescue him. The Midrash portrays the princess who comes out of the royal palace to wade in the river as a troubled person — perhaps by the idolatries and materialism of the royal court. Perhaps she is even troubled enough to show psychosomatic symptoms.

Descending into the river, she spies the little boat in the reeds, and she reaches out or perhaps sends her serving girl to take the boat. It does not appear that she knows what is in the boat at first; but she knows what is happening in Egypt, and her interest is aroused. It probably takes an effort to get hold of the little boat, but the princess is interested and determined.

When she takes the cover off, the baby begins to cry. She may have expected a newborn infant, and she seems surprised to see a three-month-old. As she perceives that a desperate Hebrew woman has left her child in that basket, praying for the best, her compassion is aroused. Moses' guardian sister leaves her hiding place and approaches to suggest that the princess take a wet nurse from among the Hebrew women. The princess agrees, perhaps afraid to trust an Egyptian woman with a Hebrew child, and the little girl, of course, brings Moses' own mother. It is not clear whether the princess knows who the woman actually is. In any event, she has Moses' own mother suckle him, but he grows up in the palace as the princess's son. The dedication that the princess shows to this Hebrew boy, even in the face of her father's decree, seems to enter deeply into Moses' own character, for he will later dedicate his whole life to serving God and the people of Israel.

THE STORY OF BITHIA expresses the strong need that many women have of living simply and fully and expressing their love and devotion in a way that is unencumbered by great material trappings. Many men do not understand this need and instead make the mistake of trying to win the love of their wives and daughters — or placate them — with wealth and comforts. Some women in such relationships may give up the possibility of being understood by men and may settle for and fixate on material possessions. In the words of a famous song of our modern culture, "Diamonds are a girl's best friend." The story of Bithia teaches a greater truth: that such a solution reflects at best a sad resignation and does not offer the sense of being involved in a divine purpose.

Bithia does not feel that diamonds are her best friend, for she willingly rejects the loveless diamonds of the pharaoh's palace to venture on a spiritual journey that better fulfills her inner character. She may be a troubled woman in her own culture, but she recognizes the emotional health in the love that Moses' sister and mother show the baby. She realizes that the poor Israelites have more of this love than the rich and powerful Egyptians do; so she leaves her home to join them. Bithia's break with her past resembles that of Abraham. She has felt herself an outsider in her native country, finding no purpose in her wealth and power. But in the Israelites' God and the closeness of their families, Bithia finds her place and purpose. Sometimes a person can feel like more of an alien in her native country and culture than in one she comes to adopt for spiritual and moral purposes.

Rizpah (II Samuel 21)

The twenty-first chapter of II Samuel tells the story of Rizpah bat Aiah, who had been a concubine to King Saul and who showed extraordinary devotion and kindness to her sons under hopeless conditions. During the reign of King David, there was a period in which God did not send rain on the land of Israel for three years. The drought was God's punishment for a sin that the Israelites had committed against the Gibeonites, a Canaanite tribe that had previously become attached to the Israelite people — under rather dubious circumstances — during the time of Joshua. King Saul and his "bloodthirsty house" had killed some of these Gibeonites, whom Israel had sworn to protect, during his misguided attack on the priests of Nob, because he suspected them of helping David against him.

Years after Saul was dead, God told David, now the Israelite king, to pacify the Gibeonites. Their demand of David, in turn, was severe and cruel: though Saul was gone, they demanded that the Israelites give over seven men of Saul's family to be hanged publicly in Gibeah. David had to follow God's command, so he surrendered Saul's two sons by Rizpah, as well as five grandsons, to the Gibeonites. The Gibeonites (II Sam. 21:9) had the seven men hanged, and they left their bodies exposed.

It was a bitter and difficult time for David and his people, but they had to accept it. Rizpah, too, had to accept God's judgment and the resulting death of her sons. (After Saul's death she had married Abner, the distinguished leader and general.) Rizpah guarded the bodies of her two sons from vultures and nocturnal predatory animals for many weeks. Seeing the great strength of this woman, and being deeply moved by her devotion to her sons, King David brought the remains of King Saul and Saul's son Jonathan from Jabesh Gilead, where they had been sequestered after they died in battle with the Philistines. The new king buried the dead king and his son with great honors, along with the seven new bodies, in the tomb in Zela of Kish, Saul's father. God was pleased with the Israelites' respect for Saul; he heard the prayers of the people and sent rain.

WE HAVE DISCUSSED A GREEK STORY (see chapter 2) that offers a strange parallel to Rizpah's story. Antigone's two brothers killed each other in battle, one defending his city and the other attacking it. King Creon, who was the uncle of both Antigone and her brothers, decreed that the brother who fell defending his city should be buried with all honors; the body of the attacking brother would be left unburied. Antigone refused to accept the king's decree and buried her second brother; because of this, the king condemned her to be locked up in a cave. When King Creon changed his mind and ordered her to be freed, his men opened the mouth of the cave — only to find Antigone dead by her own hand.

Like Rizpah, Antigone was a woman of courage and principle. However, she was also impelled by a sense of the closeness of death — even a longing for it. She was the daughter of the incestuous marriage of Oedipus and Jocasta, and she could never separate herself from the destiny of self-destruction. In a very troubling speech, Antigone declares that she would have left a husband or child unburied, for they could be replaced by another; but a brother could not be replaced if one's parents were dead (Sophocles, *Antigone*, ll. 909-13). And we should not forget that, for Antigone, Oedipus is both father and brother. The contrast with Rizpah could not be clearer: the latter is a positive biblical woman, and Antigone is a tragic Greek heroine.

45

The story of Rizpah portrays the humanity and faith of a mother whose two children have been taken from her. A mother cannot possibly experience a greater loss. Rizpah obviously grieves, yet she does not become bitter or hateful, and she guards her sons in death as she did in life. She does not turn against David because she realizes that this is a divine decree rather than one of David's plots. David recognizes the profound nature of her devotion and respects her for it. Rizpah does not see her sons as replaceable or as extensions of herself; nor does she treat them as the basis for acts of vengeance, as do the women of Greek literature such as Medea, who kills her own sons in revenge against her estranged husband Jason.

Rizpah understands that her sons have been arbitrarily caught in a divine retribution. The nobility of her reaction keeps the damage from becoming worse. Life being what it is, a woman can expect to experience loss; the question that emerges is how she will handle it. It is an error to measure a woman's suffering by her destructiveness. Rizpah retains her deep humanity — even in sorrow.

Bathsheba (II Samuel 11–12)

Bathsheba is at the center of three biblical stories. In each one she plays an important yet unobtrusive part — almost a passive part. Yet the remarkable quality of her humanity draws her to the attention of kings, princes, and prophets; and she fascinates the modern reader as well.

The first story is told in II Samuel 11. The sleepless King David is walking on the roof of his palace one night when he spots a very beautiful woman bathing in a nearby home. He learns that she is Bathsheba and that her husband, Uriah the Hittite, is encamped with General Joab's army at the siege of Rabat-Ammon. David has her brought to the palace and begins an affair with her. She becomes pregnant, and David then arranges for Uriah to be sent home for a short vacation so that everyone can assume that Bathsheba is pregnant with her husband's child. But Uriah refuses to go to his own home out of loyalty to his countrymen who are at the siege of Rabat-Ammon. When King David asks him why he has not gone home to his wife, but has slept with David's servants, Uriah says essentially: "How can I do such a thing when my comrades are on the battlefield?" David even has him stay a couple of extra days and gets him drunk; yet Uriah still sleeps with David's servants rather than going home to Bathsheba.

David is becoming a bit desperate. How can he get this honorable man to sleep with his own wife? Finally he sends a message to General Joab — via this same poor, doomed Uriah! — to place him in the most dangerous part of the battle and then have the rest of the army retreat, thus assuring that he will be struck down. Joab follows the king's orders, and Uriah is soon killed. This solves the husband problem; after granting Bathsheba an appropriate mourning period, David takes her as his wife, and in due time she gives birth to a son. But God is angry with David and causes the infant to die. David is chastened by this turn of events: he acknowledges his sins and prays for the child. His love of God is so great that, even when he has behaved badly, he still longs to be close to God. Indeed, God accepts David's repentance and forgives him, and David is able to comfort Bathsheba and restore her confidence and will to live. They have another son, Solomon, and God signifies his approbation by giving the child a special name: Jedediah, beloved of God.

The second Bathsheba story is narrated in I Kings 1. Years have passed, and David is now an aged man; he is still wise and able, but somewhat removed from daily affairs. At this point David's son Adonijah, seeing that his father's strength is waning, decides to establish himself as king, though Solomon is David's choice and God's choice. Adonijah hosts a huge feast, to which he invites many dignitaries and relatives, but not his father, nor his brother Solomon, nor Zadok the priest, nor the prophet Nathan. The guests eat and drink and hail Adonijah as king. So Nathan approaches Bathsheba and tells her about Adonijah's party, which amounts to a coup attempt. He suggests that Bathsheba go to King David and persuade him to take action. While she is with the king, Nathan says, he will come in to the presence of the king and support her plea.

Again, Bathsheba does not initiate the action, but she seems to take on the role of a person to whom one can turn for support. Her approach to David is wise beyond what even the great prophet has suggested. She comes to David's chamber and bows before him. Bowing to her husband is not usual, so David immediately realizes that something is happening, and he asks her what she needs (I Kings 1:16). Bathsheba reminds David that he has sworn in God's name that Solomon will succeed him on the throne; she even recalls David's exact words. She goes on to describe how Adonijah has already declared himself king with great fanfare — and this during David's lifetime and without even informing David. All of Israel is now looking to David to announce who will succeed him to the throne. If Adonijah does become king, he will dredge up the old story about David's affair with Bathsheba and will use it as a pretext to kill her and Solomon. She emphasizes that the "eyes of all Israel are on you to tell them who will sit on the throne of my lord the king after him" (1:20). That is, the people will follow what you tell them to do. Do not fear Adonijah, for they look to you, not to him; when Solomon sits on the throne, the people will see it as a sign that God has brought it to be.

Even as Bathsheba is speaking, Nathan arrives to confirm her words — just as they had planned. David sees the truth of their plea and takes quick action to have Solomon proclaimed king. Solomon is anointed, and Adonijah's party and coup attempt come to an abrupt end. Bathsheba's response shows that she still loves and supports David and is not looking forward to his death. She has acted with great tact and wisdom; yet she has acted through others: it is Nathan who has approached her and David who does what needs to be done.

The third story involving Bathsheba takes place soon afterward (I Kings 2). David has now died, and Solomon has peacefully assumed the crown. But Adonijah has one more card to play. He approaches Bathsheba and asks her to go to Solomon to ask that he be permitted to marry Abishag the Shunemite. This young woman had served as a nurse and companion to David in his last days; but the text emphasizes that David "knew her not." As part of his plan, Adonijah explains to Bathsheba that, after all, he almost was king, but it is clear to him that this is not God's purpose, and he accepts that fact. Yet he would like to be permitted to take Abishag the Shunemite as his wife.

Bathsheba agrees to intercede with Solomon on Adonijah's behalf. Though she is very wise and empathic in responding to people, Bathsheba here shows little political astuteness. Solomon, however, sees through Adonijah's ruse immediately. The people may think — even though it would be erroneous — that Abishag had actually been David's wife, or at least concubine, and only a king could marry a king's widow. Adonijah was thus hoping to use a marriage to Abishag as a boost to the throne. Recognizing this threat, Solomon immediately has Adonijah put to death, and he goes on to a glorious reign of forty years.

THESE THREE LINKED STORIES point to central facets of Bathsheba's personality. She is a woman who tends to see the good in people and to minimize the evil. In the first story she is drawn to David's strength and sense of purpose, even if it means accepting their illicit union. She pays the price with the death of her son. In the second story, she does not seem to be aware of Adonijah's plot to usurp the kingship. However, when Nathan warns her of the danger, it is she who persuades David to act. In the third story, Bathsheba again seems blind to Adonijah's motives; yet she informs Solomon of what Adonijah is up to next, and it is he who saves the situation.

Bathsheba seems to be a woman of great depth and empathy. She can respond to and understand a man like David in a way that his more politically shrewd wives perhaps cannot. Bathsheba can accept and feel for others. She is willing to help even Adonijah; perhaps she thinks that she could encourage the good in him and win him as a friend to Solomon. David certainly seems to find deep understanding in her. But she does not appear to be inclined toward the hurly-burly of politics. Nor is she combative or aggressive by nature. She is approachable and intelligent, and she has a beauty of character as well as of physical appearance.[1]

1. This interpretation of Bathsheba is based largely, though not wholly, on the

Hazzelelponi and Delilah (Judges 13–16)

Samson is an enigmatic figure in Scripture. He is often called "Samson the Strong" by secular thinkers and is compared to the Greek god Heracles (Hercules). Yet Scripture nowhere describes Samson as a muscular hero. His strength was a special spiritual quality given to him by God at a unique time in history. The warlike Philistines had just begun to oppress their Israelite neighbors, who lacked the weapons and armies to fight back. Samson would become a divinely appointed force who would frighten off the Philistines for some years without drawing their wrath upon his own people. He was no bumbling, muscle-bound brute like Hercules, but a man with an important mission who had to walk a tightrope: he had to hold off the Philistines while maintaining his spirituality. His story is deeply intertwined with several women, including one who was a source of his great strength — and another who caused him to lose it.

Samson's mother goes unnamed in this story in Judges, but scholars have identified her as Hazzelelponi, a woman of the tribe of Judah who is mentioned in I Chronicles 4:3. She is married to Manoah, of the tribe of Dan, a decent man but apparently less distinguished of character. The couple has been childless, but Judges 13 tells us that an angel appears to Hazzelelponi and informs her that, though she has been barren until this moment, she will soon conceive a son. Since it is possible that there has been tension between her and Manoah because of their childlessness, the angel seeks to restore peace to the household: the angel tells Hazzelelponi that the problem has been in her, not her husband, thus encouraging her to show respect to her husband. In any case, the problem has now ended. She will bear a son, and he will have a special God-ordained mission to protect his people from the Philistine oppressors. He will be a Nazirite already in the womb, so that he will have to abstain from wine and never have his hair cut; his

---

works of Don Isaac Abarbanel, the great fifteenth-century scholar who served as minister in the governments of Portugal and Spain and knew as much about queens and kings as did any man.

mother must not drink wine herself during her pregnancy, nor eat anything unclean.

Hazzelelponi goes immediately to tell her husband the news; it is a sign of respect for him that she includes him in the good tidings. She does not tell her husband that the boy will be a Nazirite, or that he will save Israel. She repeats only what is pertinent to her husband. In doing so, she spares her husband's feelings by making it look like the angel has appeared only to her to discuss female issues. Not understanding that the visitor was an angel, Manoah wants to meet him. When the angel reappears to Hazzelelponi, she asks him to wait while she brings her husband into the conversation. This may seem less than fully respectful to an angel, but Hazzelelponi again shows great consideration for her husband's feelings. Manoah addresses his own questions to the visitor and invites him to stay and eat. The angel declines, telling the couple to offer a sacrifice to God instead. When the angel returns to heaven in a fire, Manoah realizes that their guest was indeed an angel, and he is terrified that he and his wife will die in the wake of such a sight. Hazzelelponi, however, understands the situation better and assures him that if the angel had intended to kill them, he would not have given them such good news.

Hazzelelponi does not consider herself too good for her husband, even though she appears to be the stronger personality. She includes him in the prophecy she has received and even asks the angel to wait for him. Thus she exemplifies characteristics of true modesty and receptiveness: she is far-sighted and wise, not a seeker of ephemeral pleasures and honors. She is the kind of woman who not only brings out the best in herself, but in others as well. The goodness of such a woman brings light to those around her, unlocks their creativity, and in making others stronger develops her own creative qualities to their fullest.

Samson's second wife ("And Samson loved a woman in the valley of Sorek, and her name was Delilah," Judg. 16:4) is a stark contrast to his mother, and this part of the story of Samson is a good reminder that sometimes men do not have the best judgment in choosing their mates. This marriage is not part of Samson's single-handed war against the Philistines. Scripture informs us that "Samson *loved* Delilah." He is no longer a young man, and he is certainly not ignorant about the ways of the world — but he loves her. Scripture never actually says whether Delilah is an Israelite or a Philistine (perhaps it doesn't matter), though she makes a deal with the Philistines to trick Samson. Delilah may indeed have loved Samson, too, but marriage to a public figure who is always on the fringe of danger, as Samson was, cannot have been easy.

We should point out that Delilah does not seek out the Philistine lords *(serens)*. They come to her, offering a huge bribe to find out the secret of her husband's strength and apparently assuring her that they will not kill him — only capture him. Perhaps Delilah hesitates, but money suppresses many objections, and she convinces herself that cooperating with the *serens* is the right thing to do — that Samson will not be hurt much. Constantly interrogating and tormenting him, she manages to wring from him the information that his great strength is a gift from God for which his Nazirite vows are the constant reminder. Delilah arranges to have Samson's hair cut while she is holding him, weakening him so that he can be captured, blinded, and enslaved by the Philistines.

Hazzelelponi is a woman of noble character who is fit to see angelic revelations and to be chosen by God to be the mother of Samson. Considering that her devotion to her husband is exemplary, it appears that she would have been a devoted mother to Samson. Delilah shows different traits: she negotiates with the Philistines behind Samson's back, and she is seduced by their enormous bribes. With Samson she is pushy and demanding, exploiting his love for her rather than encouraging and supporting his mission. She manipulates and harasses Samson to his downfall, and she even torments him once he has been weakened.

THIS STORY ILLUSTRATES two kinds of women. The first, Hazzelelponi, is the kind of woman who sees and appreciates a man for himself. She encourages him to develop his talents and find his way — not out of personal gain for herself but because she loves him in a nonmanipulative way. Delilah is a different kind of woman: she does not support her husband in his special abilities or in his divinely appointed mission. Instead, she uses all her wiles to break down his defenses and disable him. Delilah may very well have loved Samson; that is not necessarily the problem. But her love is compromised by her willingness to sacrifice her man for her own greedy interests, and this leads her to the depths of disloyalty. Perhaps she fears that, if she were to love Samson fully, her interests would be ignored, and this is why she holds back, always calculating and never giving herself fully. Hazzelelponi does not have this fear of the future: she looks ahead to a future enlivened by God's purpose for her life, which the angel has announced to her, knowing that with God's help she will fulfill God's plan and covenant.

CHAPTER 4

True and False Wisdom

"Reverence for God is the beginning of wisdom" (Ps. 111:10) is one of the most challenging verses in all of Scripture. It does not mean that one should not think, but it does distinguish true wisdom, which emerges out of a relationship with God, from false wisdom, which is estrangement from God as is represented by the offer of the serpent in the Garden of Eden.

Women and men can show complementary kinds of wisdom. Adam, for example, may be more morally grounded than Eve, but at the same time he may be less open to experience. By contrast, Eve may be more open but less grounded. The two wise women whom David's general Joab encounters seem quite different from each other: one brings peace between David and Absalom, while the other urges the decapitation of the rebel Sheba. But they are similar in that each goes to the emotional heart of an issue rather than being paralyzed by tangential considerations. The women of the Tabernacle seem better able than are the men to connect their spiritual life with concrete action. Finally, Huldah is able to talk in a very straightforward way to King Josiah; furthermore, she grasps the emotional significance of his sending a messenger to her rather than coming to her himself.

Eve and the Fruit (Genesis 3)

The beauties of the Garden of Eden, where God has placed the newly created Adam and Eve, do not prove decisive in their lives: despite these beauties, Eve succumbs to the temptation of the serpent and eats of the forbidden fruit. And she gives it to her husband as well. The first two people do not make an adequate effort to face up to their disobedience, so God acts to change their lives in a way that will help each of them to go on living, growing, and recovering their closeness to him. God assures the woman that her greatest gift will not be taken away: she can still bear and raise children. But it will involve more pain (Gen. 3:16): "And to the woman he said, 'I will greatly increase your pain and travail. In pain you shall bear children.'" She can still have a life filled with creativity and important accomplishments, but it will take harder work than before. Because Adam has heeded his wife rather than God, it will be harder for him as well: "Cursed is the ground for your sake: in toil shall you eat of it all the days of your life. In the sweat of your face shall you eat bread, till you return to the ground" (3:17-18).

It is instructive to examine the chain of events a bit more closely. The serpent speaks only to Eve (3:1-5), and it is Eve who tempts Adam (3:6). There is no reported conversation between the serpent and Adam. God — not the serpent — is the one who speaks to Adam. The serpent has promised an easy way to knowledge by eating the forbidden fruit; this promise is interesting in that it fits in with a pagan belief in magic, but it makes no sense from a biblical point of view. It requires a belief that the fruit, when ingested, would possess magical powers and could then substitute for the knowledge of life that God has willingly given Adam and Eve. The serpent focuses on Eve, who believes its claims and subsequently convinces Adam to join her in disobeying God's command. However, the first people find the serpent's promise of quick wisdom to be greatly exaggerated. Now life will teach them that most good things, especially real human growth, require obedience to God and great effort as well.

The second part of God's injunction to Eve addresses her relationship with Adam. Clearly, the two people have hurt both themselves and one another: Adam has blamed Eve for the mess he's now in, and Eve blames the serpent. But God intends to save their relationship. His words to Eve help her define the problem she now has with her husband as well as with herself. She has given her husband the fruit because she is anxious about facing God without him. Her fear that God may take her away from her husband has led to mistaken thinking.

Now God wants Eve to understand how best to relate to Adam, so he says to her: "And to your husband will be your desire, and he shall rule over you" (3:16). It is not God's intent for husbands to dominate their wives. God does not here tell Eve to bow to Adam; rather, he is explaining to Eve an important idea. Eve seems to feel some conflict in her relationship with her husband: she needs him and depends on him in certain matters, and yet she seeks some feeling of independence as well. These two needs are not contradictory, but she must learn to find a wise balance — that is, to be a helpmeet-opposite to him. She must learn how to live life as a full person in relationship with her husband. Similarly, Adam must not ignore Eve's needs and desires, but he must coordinate his wishes with hers.

THE MAN AND WOMAN of creation each need to learn who he or she is and who his or her spouse is. Eve has a wonderful openness and attentiveness to the world around her, but she is also impressionable. She has a special way of relating to beauty and enjoying the wonder of creation; and she has a yearning for knowledge as well. Yet these characteristics lack some balance and restraint: she has succumbed to the serpent's false promises that she will both gain wisdom and experience beauty by eating the fruit that God has forbidden. The serpent chooses to speak to Eve, not to Adam, because Adam is more cautious. Eve needs more of Adam's caution and restraint to safeguard her openness, just as Adam needs more of Eve's openness to support and balance his own growth. "He shall rule over you" is not an order for Eve to be subservient to Adam; rather, it is a caution to her that she can best develop what is good and creative in herself by interacting with her husband in a healthy way. On the other side, Adam can also fulfill himself only with the support of his helpmeet-opposite.

What Eve learns from God helps her to emerge from this difficult experience as a wiser and more productive person. Adam recognizes her new growth and importance in the new name that he gives her at this time. At first he called her simply "woman, because she was taken out of man" (Gen. 2:23): that initial name, "woman," was a generic term corresponding to Adam's own self-definition as the first generic man. Now, by changing her name to "Eve, because she [is] the mother of all living" (3:20), Adam identifies his wife as going beyond a generic prototype. Eve is a true and mature human being, a wife and mother-to-be, deeply loved by both God and by her husband.

Adam's caution and restraint may have protected him from the serpent, but it also may have blocked him from connecting to some of the greatness of God's world, which Eve's responsiveness and sensitivity opens to him. While Eve may need Adam's moral strength, Adam equally needs Eve's openness to experience. Man and woman need each other. Men may sometimes be more grounded in reality than women are, but they may also be more closed to experience; by the same token, women may sometimes be more open to experience but also may be less grounded. As a couple, Adam and Eve can blend both restraint and openness, both resoluteness and sensitivity. Such blending depends on whether both humans accept the interdependence between them. This acceptance — with the addition of mutual respect — is essential to the trust necessary to make a successful relationship.

Joab and the Two Wise Women (II Samuel 14 and 20)

The book of II Samuel recounts two stories about Joab, David's great general, and women referred to simply as "wise women."

(1) David had a number of children by his various wives and concubines. Polygyny was permitted in the law of the Hebrew Bible, though it is difficult to judge today how widely it was practiced. But it clearly gave rise to complex relationships between wives and among their offspring. One of David's sons, Absalom, was a handsome and talented man whose mother was Maacah, a daughter of King Tolmi of

Geshur. Absalom killed his half-brother Amnon (another of David's sons, whose mother was Ahinoam of Jezreel) as an act of revenge: Amnon had raped Absalom's full sister Tamar. Absalom then fled to his maternal grandfather, King Tolmi, and remained in Geshur for three years.

David loved Absalom and was concerned about him, but he was also very angry with him. In this narrative in II Samuel 14, Joab wants to persuade David to invite Absalom back home, but he knows that talking to David directly about this matter will do no good. So he seeks out a "wise woman" from the town of Tekoah and tells her what he wants. The woman devises a complex play to act out before David in order to persuade him that allowing Absalom to return is the right thing to do. Dressed as a widow to stir David's compassion, she approaches him as a supplicant, weeping and saying, "Save, O King" (14:4). She claims that she is a widow in dire circumstances, and that no other court or police can help her. One of her sons has killed the other in an argument; it was not premeditated, and there were no witnesses. Yet some relatives, acting as vigilantes, now want to avenge the murder of her one son by killing her other son. But their real motivation is to claim her inheritance for themselves. If both her sons are killed, she tells King David, nothing will remain of her late husband, and it will be as though her own light has been extinguished.

David is responsive: he tells her that she should go home because he will take care of the matter. But the woman presses her petition: Will the king indeed take on this responsibility? King David assures her that, if anyone troubles her, he will take care of it. Still, she presses her petition a third time: she asks the king to warn the avengers specifically not to harm her son. David swears in God's name that no hair of her son's head will be harmed.

The wise woman then asks the king's permission to raise another matter, and when David grants it, she proceeds to explain how the case symbolized the situation of Absalom. Does the king really believe, she asks, that the Israelites will act as badly as the vigilantes in her story? In any event, people will not believe that the king has helped her since he has not brought back his own son. This is all a means of showing the king that his own exiled son needs to be brought home. "If Absalom is to be punished," she says, "let it be by God and not by the king. The king has judged my plea with the wisdom of an angel of the Lord. Now use good judgment again, and God will be with you."

By this time David understands that it must be Joab who has sent this wise woman of Tekoah to him. The woman compliments the king on his wisdom and tells him that Joab has indeed sent her. Though David himself is a very wise man, she had been wise enough to persuade him with her bit of theater. The wise woman succeeds in her efforts, and Absalom is reconciled with David — at least for a time.

(2) Hardly is Absalom's later rebellion against King David subdued when a new trouble arises in the form of Sheba, son of Bichri, a wicked man who claims that David is not divinely appointed as king, that his father Jesse was not of a royal line, and that the people of Israel should abandon David (II Samuel 20). Rebellion threatens anew, and David sends troops under Joab and Abishai to pursue Sheba, who takes refuge in Abel Beth Maacah, a fortified town. While Joab's men begin to build mounds to attack Abel and also begin to use battering rams on the walls, "a wise woman" calls to Joab from the wall. She chides him for hurrying to attack a city that has been "peaceful and faithful to Israel" without first offering terms of peace. Joab replies emphatically: "Far be it, far be it from me that I should swallow or destroy" (20:20).

Joab tells the woman that, if Abel Beth Maacah will simply give up Sheba, who has rebelled against King David, David's troops will leave the city in peace. The woman promises that Sheba's head will soon be thrown over the wall to Joab. The people of Abel are reluctant, not knowing whether this is the right thing to do. But the wise woman persuades them that the whole city is in danger if they do not do it — that Sheba is a rebel and has to be given up. So they cut off Sheba's head and throw it over the wall to Joab, who blows his trumpet and withdraws his army. The woman's wisdom and courage have saved her city.

THE STORIES of the two "wise women" describe two seemingly opposite reactions. The first wise woman intervenes to bring peace between David and Absalom; the second urges the decapitation of the rebel

Sheba to appease David and his general, Joab. Yet their aims are similar. Each woman is trying to preserve the stability and welfare of her community.

It is significant that women play the central roles in these two stories. The wise woman of Tekoah uses a parable to make her point; but she embeds that parable within a play, rather than expressing it didactically — as biblical prophets often did (see Nathan's parable regarding David's taking of Bathsheba in II Samuel 12:1-14). The Tekoah sage is able to create an emotional context that engages David's interest in a way that most men could not. The wise woman of Abel Beth Maacah acts quickly and decisively. She understands that this is no time to philosophize; instead, she needs to go right to the heart of the matter to save her city. In each of these biblical stories, it is a woman who knows what to do and is not paralyzed by tangential considerations. Both narratives portray women of great strength and wisdom, and it is a wise man who encourages that.

Women in the Tabernacle (Exodus 32–38)

Women played a vital role in the building of the Tabernacle in the Sinai Desert after the exodus from Egypt. They did much of the handicraft work and contributed essential materials. Exodus 38:8 says that women gave their personal mirrors for the construction of the great water basin. "He made the basin of copper and its base of copper from the mirrors of the women who had gathered at the entrance of the Tabernacle." And it appears that women preceded the men in donating their material items: "And the men came along after the women" (Exod. 35:22). Also, "the wise-hearted women spun with their own hands and they brought spun yarn of blue and purple and scarlet wool and linen. And all the women whose hearts raised them up in wisdom spun the goats' hair" (35:25-26).

It becomes apparent that the women were especially devoted to building the tabernacle and to its worship; every day a certain number of women "gathered at the entrance" to pray and to study the commandments. They contributed their gold and jewels as well as their mirrors, brooches, nose rings, earrings, and signet rings (35:22). Mirrors and jewels would seem to be objects useful only for human vanity, not holiness; yet they were accepted as suitable materials for building the Tabernacle and its vessels because of the great respect God had for the women's courage and faith in maintaining their families under the bitter conditions of the Egyptian bondage. On the other hand, when the Israelites formed and worshiped the golden calf in the desert, it appears that the men contributed far more readily to the idolatry, while the women gave only when forced. "And Aaron said to them [the men]: 'Break off the golden rings which are in the ears of your wives, of your sons and your daughters and bring them to me'" (Exod. 32:2).

The women understood very well how important their role had been and still was, and they aided the Tabernacle more readily and more generously than did the men. The women's devotion to the service of the Tabernacle was perhaps rooted in their pious devotion to God and perhaps equally rooted in their understanding of how important this service was for protecting the spiritual welfare of their families.

WOMEN OFTEN UNDERSTAND more fully than do men the importance of the physical manifestations of the sacred. A man may feel that the spiritual and intellectual part is enough, and he can be irritated by tangible obligations. Women seem to realize more readily that without physical practices the spiritual beliefs can fade away over the course of a generation or two. Thus the women's great attention to the Tabernacle may have been the wisest response to the debacle of the golden calf. The Tabernacle provided both a concrete and a spiritual anchor that a purely spiritual belief could not.

It can be argued that many of the ritual laws of the Hebrew Bible are directed more toward men than toward women. The Talmud declares that women are freed from fulfilling positive commandments related to time. A woman's life is by its very nature time-centered — for example, in the bearing and rearing of children — in a way that a man's is not. Much of Greek and Western misogyny reflects a defense against time, and this derives from the Platonic elevation and idealization of the timeless and the eternal, as opposed to the time-bound realities of daily life.

Huldah (II Kings 22)

In Jerusalem's Second Temple complex, a chamber called Huldah's Gate was attached to the outer wall. The name commemorated the prophetess Huldah, who had occupied a similar chamber centuries before during the reign of the righteous King Josiah in the waning days of the First Temple, difficult times for the kingdom of Judah. Josiah's grandfather, King Manasseh, had turned to idol worship and had persecuted the prophets of the true God. He was forced to pay heavy tribute to the emperors of Assyria and was himself carried off as a captive. Manasseh tried to improve matters when he returned, but he had already done much damage. His reign of fifty-five years — longer than the reigns of David or Solomon — left Judah morally weakened. His grandson Josiah became king at the age of eight; and as Josiah grew older, he began to pay serious attention to the moral decay of Judah, making serious efforts to repair God's Temple and to stimulate the people's interest in the teachings of the Torah. One day, the workers repairing the Temple found the copy of the Pentateuch that had been written by Moses himself. They brought the scroll to King Josiah, and he had Shafan, the scribe, open it and read it to him. What the latter read was the passage in Deuteronomy that describes the fearful destruction and exile that would come upon the Israelites if they were to stray from fulfilling their duties to God and man.

A deeply sincere and upright man, Josiah was so moved by the words that he tore his garments as a sign of contrition, and he decided to seek advice. The great prophet Jeremiah was active at that time, but King Josiah did not turn to him. Scholars have suggested that perhaps Jeremiah was away at the moment of Josiah's seeking; but perhaps Josiah simply felt that the times needed another kind of understanding and empathy. In any event, he consulted the prophetess Huldah, who occupied her chamber on the Temple grounds and gave forth teachings and advice. Strangely, her name can be translated as "weasel," though this did not seem to reflect her spiritual and intellectual powers.

King Josiah sent a delegation to inquire of God "for my sake and the people's sake and for Judah over the words of the Book, for great is the anger of God burning against us because our fathers did not heed the words of this Book" (II Kings 22:13). So Hilkiah the priest, accompanied by Ahikam, Akhbor, Shafan, and Asaiah, went to Huldah. The names Akhbor and Shafan can be translated, respectively, as "rat" and "badger." The use of these two names, along with Huldah's name (weasel), is curious: Could this indicate a period of such low confidence that it caused people to give their children names that seem so unpromising?

In any event, if King Josiah was hoping for a more optimistic answer from Huldah, he did not receive it. She may have even been a bit offended that the king did not come himself. "So says the Lord God of Israel, 'Say to the man who sent you . . .'" (22:15) — not "to your royal master" or "to the King." God will indeed bring all the evils on the land and its inhabitants as the book that the king had read to him foretells. "My anger burns, and it will not cease" (22:17). Yet God has seen the sincere repentance of King Josiah and how he rent his garment and wept. Therefore, according to Huldah's prophecy, Josiah will be gathered to his fathers in peace and will not see all the evils that God will bring on Judah.

THIS STORY REFLECTS a uniquely biblical view of women. Neither mindless nor cruel, Huldah feels compassion toward Josiah, but she talks to him straight. First, she lets the king know that she feels he should have come himself rather than sending a messenger. This is not simply her expression of personal annoyance at a social affront: she wants Josiah to step into her world and be fully involved so that she can talk to him directly.

Huldah senses that the king's not visiting her reflects how bad the situation really is. Although he is a good man, he cannot rectify the problems in Judah. Her advice, while seemingly harsh, is deeply honest and compassionate. She tells the messenger that the situation is indeed threatening, but that Josiah is a good man. Not every man, no matter how well intended he may be, is capable of meeting every external challenge, and the prophetess can berate him for this or accept him. She accepts him, recognizing both his limitations and his essential goodness. She prophesies that Josiah will die in peace, not having to witness the calamitous destruction of the kingdom that is certain to come.

CHAPTER 5

Courage

Western literature praises courage, most readily associating it with warriors in battle. The Hebrew Bible also loves courage, but it does not recognize it only in those who face enemy armies. In many instances biblical women acted with a courage that was based not on weapons and brawn but on wisdom and faith in the divine purpose: "Not in the power of the horse is his desire, and not in the man's legs is he pleased" (Ps. 147:10). Courage often expresses itself quietly, in small and almost unnoticed acts that can lead to unexpected but significant results. This is the kind of courage that is displayed not only in one moment of danger and heroics but as an act that forms a pattern in a mosaic of good works. We find such heroics in the stories of the midwives who defied the pharaoh's murderous pronouncement during the Hebrew captivity in Egypt that is recorded in this chapter.

Abigail, too, acts not only with courage in a very dangerous moment but also with great political skill. Perhaps the most noble kind of courage is expressed in the verses in Proverbs 31 that describe the "woman of valor": "She smiles at the final day." Moses' sister Miriam was also a person whose courage expressed itself in many situations. This chapter tells of an instance in which Miriam was wrong, but where she was no less respected and beloved for her error.

Miriam and the Cushite Woman (Numbers 12)

Moses had the greatness to bring the well of water out of the rock by himself. Yet without Miriam, he could do so only by force, hitting the rock with his staff. Miriam supplied unique wisdom and ability within her family and to the people of Israel — both in Egypt and during the journey through the Sinai wilderness. Numbers 12 tells the story of one of a series of challenges to the truth of Moses' prophetic mission. First there were other prophets, such as Eldad and Medad. Then the spies challenged Moses' ability to lead the Israelites into the promised land of Canaan. Korah challenged both Moses' role as leader and the reality of the God-given law.

But in this narrative in Numbers 12, Miriam, for whom the children and family life of her people were so important, seems to have become disturbed at the lack of Moses' relationship with his own wife and their two sons since his marriage to a Cushite woman. Moses' level of interaction with God is unique and unquestioned; but his wife and children appear to be lacking his attention, and Miriam's concern is focused on them. She voices her concerns to their brother Aaron, and then apparently to Moses himself. God then intervenes, replying that Moses is fulfilling his mission at a higher level than any other human being, and that his work is so important that it must take precedence over family: "In all my house he [Moses] is trusted." Moses is unique in standing face to face with God.

Miriam is correct in saying that other leaders and prophets, including herself, should not separate themselves from day-to-day life. Yet Moses has learned to rise above mundane needs, even of food, for example, when he spent forty days learning from God on the mountain. In a sense, this is comparable to a scientist who foregoes daily pleasures and even meals to spend days and nights in his lab, where he is totally devoted to seeking a cure for a disease. He may save a multitude of lives, but he may lose something in the interaction with his family along the way. For many years Moses devoted himself completely to rescuing the children of Israel from Egyptian bondage and then to receiving the law from God and teaching it to his people.

A second woman is mentioned in Numbers 12, but her identity is debatable: "And Miriam and Aaron spoke . . . for he had married a Cushite woman." Commentators have found this puzzling. Who was this woman? Wasn't Moses married to Zipporah, daughter of Jethro the Midianite? One ancient story is repeated by a number of medieval writers and is also told by the historian Josephus in the first century. As a young man still living in Pharaoh's court, Moses killed an Egyptian overseer for brutalizing an Israelite slave. Moses fled from Egypt to Ethiopia, where he became a great warrior king and married a local (i.e., Ethiopian, or Cushite) princess. Then, some years later, Moses came to Midian, where he married Zipporah. Some commentators question this view: Why is it that only now, years after the event, Miriam and Aaron bring up this story? The word "Cushite" may refer to a particular nation and describe the woman's origin; but some are of the opinion that the word means "beautiful" and that it actually does refer to Zipporah. Miriam may have been questioning why Moses did not pay more attention to a wife who was so refined and attractive.

Moses never loses his love for his elder sister, even at the moment she criticizes him. When God punishes her with *tsora'at* (a disease that affects the skin, among other things), Moses quickly pleads with God to heal her. The people of Israel love and respect Miriam as well, and they delay their journey a full week, until she is restored to health.

THIS STORY ILLUSTRATES the essential complementarity of men and women. Men and women are different, and they see strength, development, and fulfillment differently. Moses' highest calling came after many years as a husband and father. He had to remove himself from familial cares to always be open to God's call to him. It is not that he does not love his wife and children or that he rejects them; but he knows that some separation is essential to enable him to fulfill his special mission from God. Miriam's understanding is different: it involves a man being deeply involved in the life of his family. She is not unappreciative of Moses' special calling, but she feels that he must not sacrifice the needs of his wife and children.

God shows the rectitude of Moses in this issue when he afflicts

Miriam with *tsora'at,* an impurity that makes it impossible for her to encounter God directly in worship in the Tabernacle, something Moses could not allow to befall him at this stage of his mission. Miriam and Moses are not really polarized here. Moses is not antagonistic toward his family, and Miriam does not fail to appreciate Moses' unique work. Each accepts much of what the other is saying. Yet, just as she did when the Israelites crossed the Red Sea, Miriam sings her own song. She is not intimidated, nor does she reject God or Moses to express her point. It does not detract from her greatness that in this instance God judged Moses to be right.

Abigail (I Samuel 25)

David's life was an unusual combination of action, intellect, and deep feeling. Yet all of this could have been destroyed — and he almost did self-destruct on more than one occasion — had he not been saved by the intervention of a wise woman several times. Abigail, blessed with unusual wisdom and beauty, lived in Maon with her husband, Nabal, a man who had great wealth but was insolent and ill-mannered. In those days David was not yet enthroned as the king of Israel; he was a fugitive pursued by King Saul. A band of four hundred men gathered around David, and they hid near Maon, where they gave protection and help to Nabal's shepherds in the wilderness. As they were running short on supplies, David heard that Nabal would be giving a huge feast, and he sent a messenger to Nabal, asking respectfully for food and reminding Nabal of the services to his shepherds. Nabal, however, responded with his customary churlishness: "Who is David and who is the son of Jesse? Today, too many slaves are breaking out against their masters. Shall I take my bread, my water, and my meat, which I have prepared for my shearers, and give it to men whom I do not know from whence they come?" (I Sam. 25:10-11).

That the prophet Samuel had already anointed David to succeed Saul was well known among the Israelites; and, in any case, Nabal's reply treated David as if he were a slave. In a towering rage, David tells his men to strap on their swords, and they head out toward Maon. One of Nabal's young workers comes to tell Abigail how helpful David's men have been to the shepherds: "And the men were very good to us. . . . They were a wall for us both night and day, while we were with them watching the sheep" (25:15-16). But now, he says, Nabal is putting them all in great danger: "Know and see what you can do, because evil is coming on our master and all his house, and he is an ill-tempered man to whom one cannot talk" (25:17).

Blessed with great wisdom, Abigail realizes that there is plenty of food for the celebration and that large amounts can be removed without being missed. Abigail acts immediately, sending elaborate food supplies ahead to David with her workers and following not far behind them herself. David and his men are on the way to Maon, their rage building as they march. Then, unexpectedly, here are the food supplies, and then Abigail. Hurrying off her donkey and bowing to David, she takes the blame for what has happened. Abigail asks David not to overreact to Nabal's insolence. She changes the perspective: it would surely be God, not Abigail, who can hold David back from a major mistake. She says, in effect, God is helping you build a true house and kingship, and no one, including Nabal, can harm you. You have always fought God's battles, and no fault is to be found with you, even in your behavior as a fugitive from King Saul. May God fulfill all his plans for you and your kingdom. "Now let this not be a stumbling block . . . for my master to shed blood to no purpose" (25:31).

Abigail points out to David that, if he massacres Nabal's household, he will create an ugly incident that will plague him all through his reign, and he will never be able to rule without the shadow of these murders. David recognizes the wisdom and truth in Abigail's words and respects the wise woman who has saved him from a terrible mistake. "Blessed is the God of Israel, who sent you to meet me today and blessed is your wisdom and blessed are you who stopped me from bloodshed" (25:32-33). David sees that Abigail is entirely correct. He accepts the supplies she has brought as a gift and promises to turn his men back.

When Abigail returns home, Nabal is so thoroughly drunk at his sheep-shearing feast that she will have no success in her effort to speak to him. However, the next morning, when Abigail tells Nabal what has happened, he is struck by a serious attack, perhaps heart failure or a stroke, either because he could not tolerate giving away the food or because he is shocked to learn about the danger that has been so narrowly averted. Nabal lingers ten days and then dies. David is relieved to hear that God has judged this arrogant man and has saved his own hand from wrongdoing. In due course, David takes the widow Abigail as his wife, and their son Kileab grows up to be a wise and righteous man.

THIS STORY VIVIDLY ILLUSTRATES a difference in strength between a man and a woman. When a man feels wronged, he often becomes possessed of an intolerable rage and will overreact in ways that are inimical to his long-term interests. Perhaps this is intrinsic to male psychology. This may explain the attraction of men to fierce competitive sports such as football, rugby, and boxing. Often in responding to an affront, a man's action can become so violent that it overrides the inherent righteousness of his acts. David's anger at Nabal's arrogant affront is understandable, but his planned response is so extreme as to obscure that fact.

Enter Abigail, an equally strong personality, who basically agrees with David's judgment concerning her husband's behavior. However, she has a woman's sense of restraint, which enables her to cool him down and show him how his planned action will hamper God's plans for him. It is to David's credit that he is open to listening to her. Not so her churlish husband, who should have been happy that Abigail has saved his life. Unlike David, he could not listen; perhaps he could not tolerate being one-upped by his wife, though her intervention has, in fact, saved him. David can recognize and accept a strong and courageous woman, while Nabal cannot. In this, David reflects the attitude toward women of a biblical man, while Nabal's attitude reflects that of the macho pagan male who is unsure of his manhood.

Shifra and Puah (Exodus 1)

Two women described as "God-fearing" are the midwives in Exodus 1 whose names, or perhaps titles, were Shifra and Puah. Fearing the rapid natural population increase of the Israelites in the land Egypt controlled, the Egyptians have enslaved them. Yet the Hebrew population continues to proliferate. Pharaoh wants try a new plan. He calls on two midwives who have served the Hebrew women and instructs them to see to it that the newborn male babies do not survive. Baby girls would be permitted to live, perhaps because they would be easier to absorb into Egyptian life — and they certainly would not attack Egypt once they reached maturity. Perhaps this plan seems less drastic to Pharaoh than openly massacring the Israelites.

It is likely that the two women of this story are leaders among the midwives, though it is not clear whether they are Egyptian or Hebrew. An order from Pharaoh has to be taken seriously; yet these two midwives are more concerned with God's rules than with the pharaoh's. The pharaoh soon realizes that his plan is not working and that the Israelites' numbers continue to increase anyway. Not only do the midwives not kill the boys; they help care for the newborns and nourish them. The midwives are putting themselves in great danger by doing all this; indeed, no one could have faulted them if they had let the baby boys die or simply refused to give the extra help. But these midwives did not shrink from their responsibilities, despite the great danger to themselves. God saw this and repaid them by continuing the great growth of population even in the face of hard times: "And God was good to the midwives, and the people multiplied" (Exod. 1:20).

SHIFRA AND PUAH have a biblical reverence for life that the Egyptians do not share, and they show it in their treatment of the Hebrew babies. Yet that biblical sensibility is not limited to the Israelites. Remember that Ruth, a Moabite woman, acted in every way as any biblical heroine did. Shifra and Puah behaved in a very biblical way as well: that they saved Israelite babies is not incidental, for even though they may have been Egyptians, they operated with an Israelite spirit. And this spirit and activity of liberation is not limited to ancient peoples. In the twentieth century, those who saved potential victims during the Holocaust were also operating out of a sense of biblical morality, and by doing so they were able to save some of the "people of the book."

Many of the biblical teachings and rules are addressed to all people. The concept of this story of the midwives comes out as one of the universal laws God taught Noah after the great flood: every human being, regardless of nation, is created in the image of God and is dear to God.

Woman of Valor (Proverbs 31)

The book of Proverbs has much to say about women, and, in fact, much of its very last chapter is a paean of praise to the "woman of valor." What portrait of this remarkable woman does Proverbs offer?

To begin with, a woman is, by the definition of her Creator, good: "He who has found a wife has found a good thing" (Prov. 18:22); also, "an understanding wife is a gift from God" (19:14), which implies that many people do not choose marital partners by themselves on the basis of very clear thinking. Rather, marrying a wise woman is a gift from God. A man must see his marriage as a divine gift and must approach looking for a wife by using a biblical model. In addition, "a gracious woman finds support in her honor" (11:16); that is, one of the essential qualities of a truly "gracious woman" is that she is aware of her own dignity and moral value as a human being. This dignity informs whatever she does or says. It is self-respect of the most genuine kind, and other people sense this in her and respond to it.

The valiant woman of Proverbs 31 is a treasure. Her family trusts her to always do her best for others and never to harm them for her own petty spite. She is deeply involved in the details of caring for her family and household — and for the needy as well. She feeds her family and dresses them well, and she is supportive of her husband. She is positive and cheerful and does not worry unduly about the future; instead, she plans well. She receives the gratitude of her family. Indeed, her works themselves are her praise, but that does not mean that people should not let her know she is appreciated: "Give her of the fruits of her hands, and her works will praise her in the gates" (31:31). Beauty is a blessing, and certainly the Bible notes of Sarah, Rebecca, and Rachel that they were beautiful. However, good character and closeness to God are of lasting value: "Charm is deceit and beauty is vain. A God-fearing woman is to be praised" (31:30). The woman of Proverbs 31 is wise and kind, independent and trustworthy, and with her ability and devotion she handles the details of living.

All this contrasts notably with the attitude toward women that one often finds in the literature of ancient Greece. In the sixth century B.C.E., Semonides of Amorgos wrote a poem in which he negatively portrayed a number of women, comparing them to various animals — a sow, a vixen, a dog, a monkey, and an ape. They are all miserable homemakers and unpleasant spouses. Their conversation is worthless. They are slovenly and loud, gluttonous and voracious. Only one is like the bee and a true joy to her husband. We cannot be sure today whether Semonides wrote the poem tongue-in-cheek or in anger, or perhaps as a birthday card to his wife; but his demeaning description of women is fairly typical of Greek thinking.

WESTERN CULTURE REJECTS a slovenly housewife, as does biblical culture, preferring a dignified woman. However, the meaning of dignity is different for the two. Traditional Western culture admires a woman who is a proper hostess, can raise obedient children, dresses well, and makes appropriate conversation. Her dignity is not to be soiled or diminished by sexuality or affection, by overt disagreements with her husband, or by expressing her personality. She is to be prim and proper. An alternative, often seen today, is the woman who expresses everything. This can result in overt and violent arguments with husbands and other family members for no other reason than a woman's self-assertion and refusing to adjust and to join in a common purpose.

The ideal of the "woman of valor" is neither of these extremes. She is strong and purposeful, yet modest and agreeable. Her strength comes from her understanding of who she is in her family. When she disagrees with her husband, it is in terms of the family's important goals. Her home is a warm and pleasant place to visit. It is neither overly formal nor chaotic; rather, it is a place where people like to come and enjoy the warmth and support. The description of such a woman as a gift from God is also revealing: she and her husband form a union that transcends their own concerns and becomes part of the divine plan of what marriage should be. The biblical woman's dignity must be understood in the context of devoting her talents to fulfilling this promise. She is dignified because she has not only a deep sense of purpose but also the character and wisdom to pursue it. Because she is a helpmeet-opposite, there are times when she must disagree with her husband for the good of the family. However, when she does disagree, she will do so to help the family, not to undercut or humiliate her husband. Their marriage thrives when each partner can express his or her particular talents for the common good.

CHAPTER 6

Unhealthy Sexuality

Sexuality is a healthy expression of love and intimacy between a man and a woman. "Therefore shall a man leave his father and mother and shall cleave unto his wife, and they shall become one flesh" (Gen. 2:24). Yet sexuality can also be distorted into something debasing and ugly. Perhaps the worst expression of unhealthy sexuality is when it is forced — that is, rape. Second Samuel describes the rape of Tamar by her half-brother Amnon. Amnon compounds the damage he has done to his sister by driving her away after the act, reflecting his disgust with himself. Another rape occurs in the story of Dinah, the daughter of Jacob, by the prince of Shechem. Her brothers avenge her, perhaps because of a feeling that they had not protected her sufficiently. A third story tells of the concubine of Gibeah, who is sent out by her husband to appease a gang of thugs, and who is gang-raped and murdered — with widespread and disastrous consequences.

Another example of unhealthy and distorted sexuality can be seen in the cult of temple prostitution that was so common in the ancient pagan world but forbidden in the book of Deuteronomy. The story of Cozbi illustrates again the manipulative use of sexuality, designed to entice the Israelite men into biblically prohibited idolatrous practices. Yet the narrative of Hosea about Gomer, a prostitute, stands as a parable for the possibility that people can change. God instructs the prophet Hosea to marry Gomer, and over time Hosea becomes very attached to her and brings her back into God's favor.

Tamar, Sister of Absalom (II Samuel 13)

King David was a man of deep feeling and faith who could turn a potential moral disaster into an event of great meaning, as he did in the matter of his affair with Bathsheba (see chapter 1). Yet sometimes an evil act leaves its own evil legacy, and II Samuel 13 chronicles this legacy in the story of David's family. Once immorality has entered the family chronicle, it does not simply disappear. In this story, Amnon, one of David's sons, becomes infatuated with Tamar, who is Absalom's full sister and his half sister. (The text refers to her as Amnon's sister, but the nature of their relationship is not entirely clear; she may have been David's daughter with a *Yefat Toar* [see chapter 8].) When Amnon is so lovestruck that he becomes physically ill, his friend and cousin Jonadab, a brilliant fellow, figures out what is bothering Amnon and devises a plan by which Amnon will have a chance to pour out the love in his heart to Tamar. This narrative has all the suspense and human drama of a Shakespearean plot. Perhaps rape has crossed Jonadab's mind, but he never suggests it to Amnon directly. Jonadab advises Amnon to feign illness (which doesn't take much acting since he is already lovesick) and to take to his bed. Things go as planned, and when King David comes to visit his sick son, Amnon asks that Tamar be sent over to bake cakes for him in his room. Following David's command, Tamar does come in and busies herself with the baking.

When the cakes are ready, Amnon sends everyone except Tamar out of the room. Then he asks Tamar to bring the food into his bedroom, and when she unwittingly complies, he seizes her and says, "Come lie with me, my sister." Shocked and horrified, Tamar pleads with him to let her go, offering three reasons: (1) such a "disgraceful thing" should not be done in Israel (13:12), using a term that would remind him of the story of Dinah; (2) rape would be shameful and devastating for Tamar and her future (13:13a); (3) Amnon himself, in committing such a terrible sin, would mark himself as a fool and an evil person in Israel (13:13b).

Amnon has no interest in listening to her, and seeing that she will not comply of her own free will, he forces her. Afterward, Amnon is disgusted with both himself and Tamar. "Greater was the hatred which Amnon felt toward her than the love he had felt before" (13:15). Amnon now orders Tamar to leave him, but she refuses: "Not so, because this great wrong in sending me away is worse than the other that you did to me" (13:16). This is a very important statement on the part of Tamar: it indicates that Amnon's guilt and revulsion make him hurt her even more. When Tamar does not leave quickly enough, Amnon tells his attendants to drive Tamar out and bolt the door behind her. He must get Tamar out of his sight.

Tamar, feeling broken and desolate, goes to live in the house of her full brother, Absalom, and the latter encourages her to do her best to forget what has happened. David is furious with Amnon because of his sexual assault on Tamar, but he apparently does nothing. Absalom bides his time, not speaking to Amnon. But two years later, he receives David's permission to invite Amnon and all David's other sons to a feast he is hosting for sheep-shearers in Baal-hazor. At this feast Absalom orders his servants to murder his brother Amnon (13:23-29).

The Bible goes on to narrate the story of David's problems with Absalom and the young man's rebellion against his father and his rape of some of his father's wives. Unsparing as it always is of its heroes, Scripture's main theme in this story seems to be the potentially devastating effects on both family and society of sexual sins and crimes.

A VERY IMPORTANT MESSAGE in this story is the significance of repentance and atonement in biblical thought. When someone wrongs another, as Amnon has done to Tamar, the perpetrator often hates the person he has previously loved and now has wronged because of how the action now makes him feel about himself. In Somerset Maugham's terms, there is but a "razor's edge" between love and hate. Without taking an opportunity to atone for his sin, the perpetrator will often grow to hate the person he has victimized, because the victim serves as a continuous reminder of the perpetrator's evil action.

Amnon never acknowledges his sin (as David did concerning his affair with Bathsheba), nor does he attempt to atone for it in any way. Had Amnon atoned for his act, he may well have developed compassion for Tamar, his victim, rather than compounding her suffering by his continued and perhaps even greater mistreatment of her. This story points to the biblical insistence on repentance and atonement. It is critical both for the perpetrator of misconduct as well as for its victim. Otherwise, the perpetrator will grow to hate both himself and his victim, and they both may become pariahs in the community. And as we have seen in the continuing story of Amnon and Absalom, the compounded damage to family and society can result in greater evils down the road.

Dinah (Genesis 34)

In Scripture, human sexuality is an expression of joy and intimacy between a man and a woman. It is a human need and a powerful drive that offers unique and intense pleasure. The first command and blessing God ordains for Adam and Eve is to be fruitful and multiply (Gen. 1:28). Far from being sinful in the book of Genesis, sex is on the divine to-do list. But there are also rules. Sexuality is used to express human sanctity, not to express power or control over others — and certainly not to hurt others. Rape is beyond a sexual conquest; it is a crime, a misuse and betrayal of the divine blessing, and a violation of the integrity of a human being and of all humankind. The biblical attitude toward it is in contrast to the literature of ancient Greece, which featured story after story of rape, and which treated sexuality as a matter of abuse or jest, not a joyous blessing sanctified by God himself.

The Hebrew Bible is horrified by the story of the rape of Dinah. Dinah is the central figure in the Genesis 34 story, yet she does not utter a word. A daughter of Leah and Jacob, Dinah has lived her childhood in a family that is hard-working, intelligent, and close-knit. They have migrated from Haran back to Canaan, where, after various trials, Jacob has bought a piece of land near Shechem and settled down to pasture his flocks. Jacob and his sons have had various dealings with the family of King Hamor of Shechem, from whom they acquired the land, and probably some of Hamor's people were present when Jacob dedicated a nearby altar to God. Some time has passed, and ancient sources tell us that there was a festive day in the town in which the young women went out into the streets to play music and dance. Or was it all a ploy? Shechem, King Hamor's favorite and very spoiled son, has already noticed Dinah. In his plan, she would come to watch the festivities, and he would kidnap her there. Curious about the celebration, Dinah does indeed come to the festival to watch, and Shechem carries her off by force to his palace, where he rapes her several times. No one in the city protests this act of cruelty.

Dinah's brothers have been at their work in the fields, but they come home to join Jacob and deal with King Hamor, who comes to tell them that his son Shechem loves Dinah and now wants her hand in marriage. Notice that, though young Shechem could rape the young woman by himself, when it comes to asking for her in marriage, his father has to handle it for him. King Hamor offers Jacob's family an alliance by which the two groups can intermarry and carry on commerce with each other.

Hamor reveals himself to be an immoral man: his overtures to Jacob emphasize only that "my son desires your daughter." He does not describe his son as a refined and educated young man of good character, which he clearly is not. Hamor sounds as though he feels Shechem's marriage to Dinah is beneath them; but he loves his son and will give him anything he wants. He does not apologize for the rapes. In fact, he doesn't even mention them — nor does he offer to return Dinah. It is more a matter of "when my son wants anything, he should have it."

In order to get Dinah back, Jacob's sons answer with trickery. They will consent to the marriage, they say, if all the men of Shechem will have themselves circumcised — "for we cannot do this thing and give our sister to a man with a foreskin because it is degrading for us."

The prince Shechem readily agrees, and so do the citizens, beguiled by Hamor's promises of the wealth that will come by way of this alliance with the sons of Israel (Jacob). Hamor's words to his people are hardly friendly to Israel's family: "Their cattle and all their goods, will they not be ours?" (34:23).

On the third day after the mass circumcision, when all of the men of Shechem are sore and weak, Simeon and Levi, two of Jacob's sons, take their short Mycenean swords and kill every man of Shechem, and then bring Dinah home from the palace. Although she certainly has been the victim and has done nothing wrong, Dinah is almost reluctant to go home because of the great shame she feels over what has happened. Her emotions are typical of rape victims, who find it difficult to face day-to-day life after their ordeal and find it even more difficult to talk about it. Her brothers have taken strong action to get her back, but they also blame themselves for what has happened: "And the men were grieved . . ." (34:7). Had they protected Dinah better, they thought, they might have prevented the whole terrible trauma.

It is typical that in a crisis the young men are more willing to resort to war or violence, while the old men are usually more cautious. Jacob is concerned that the massacre in Shechem may bring a violent revenge from neighbors in Canaan, but Simeon and Levi reply that they had to rescue Dinah and teach Prince Shechem and the Shechemites a lesson (34:31: "Should he treat our sister like a harlot?"). This was a crime, they said, not only against Dinah as an individual but against a people and its way of life, so it called for a decisive response. Scripture says no more about the fate of Dinah. Later literature tells several stories, including one that she lived with Simeon's family as a kind of widow. Medieval travelers tell of seeing her tomb near the town of Arbel in Galilee.

SOME CRITICS HAVE ARGUED that the Scripture assaults Dinah a second time by leaving her speechless all through the story. Underlying this criticism is the assumption that a rape victim such as Dinah must be given a place to express herself and declare her outrage, and that this biblical story degenerates into a battle of honor among men in which Dinah is reduced to a mere stick figure. Is this criticism fair? Often a victim of an assault may be unable to speak for herself and is filled with self-loathing and self-blame. Many ancient cultures would have presumed Dinah to be guilty and would have subjected her to punishment and humiliation in which she would have to proclaim her innocence through a demeaning verbal self-defense. In contrast, Dinah's brothers immediately side with her. This indicates the highest regard for her sensitivities, not a lack of respect for her. They even fight for *her*, not simply for the concept of honor, as in the Greek world; they fight for their sister, whom they accept as a full human being. Dinah does not need to defend herself, for her innocence is obvious — as is the guilt of Shechem. Nor does she need to suffer any stigma, because she has brought no shame on her family. The shame is Shechem's, not hers.

It is also possible that Dinah's family feels guilty that they have not protected her better in the hostile environment of Schechem. Better protection might have spared Dinah the entire terrible experience; and better protection would have signified, not a lack of respect for her, but a recognition of a real danger. There is often a fine line between protecting and controlling. In Dinah's case, the lack of sufficient family protectiveness led to terrible consequences for her. And perhaps the brothers were directing part of their anger against themselves for not protecting her well enough. Even seen in that perspective, though, the shame was their own and not Dinah's.

Gomer (Hosea 1–2)

The opening chapters of the prophetic book of Hosea use the imagery of a strange marriage to explain God's love of Israel. The people had sinned by seeing their God not as the loving and benevolent deity he is, but as a deity similar to the cruel Baals worshiped by the neighboring nations. The Baals had to be appeased and pacified so that they would reward their subjects and not punish those subservient to them. These non-Israelite peoples deified the wild powers of nature and fertility, and, in imitation, the Israelites had also begun to think of their God as a Baal figure rather than as a beloved parent.

In this first book of the Minor Prophets, Hosea, a learned and spiritual man, is dismayed by his own people's turning away from God. And he wonders whether God can still love this group of people who have drifted away from him. God decides to teach an important lesson, not only to Hosea but to the people of Israel as a whole — a lesson that the prophet will feel personally — about the depth of God's continuing love. God tells the prophet to marry Gomer, a well-known prostitute. Over time, Gomer has three children with the prophet, and each child is given a name that reflects the growing discord between God and his people: Jezreel, the first son's name, refers to Jehu's bloody rebellion in Jezreel; Lo-Ruhama, the daughter's name, means "no mercy"; and Lo-Ammi, the second son's name, means "not my people."

Marriage to a longtime prostitute could not have been easy for Hosea because he could never fully trust her. Yet, despite the inherent problems of such a marriage, Hosea becomes very attached to Gomer, and he would not have found it easy to send her away. This marriage, of course, parallels God's own relationship with the people of Israel. The Israelites have misunderstood God and fallen away from him, believing that his bountiful gifts to them have actually come from the Baals.

Yet, just as Hosea has come to love Gomer and does not want to give her up, despite her faults, so God continues to love his people, though they have strayed from him. At God's command, Hosea changes the names of two of his children: Lo-Ammi becomes Ammi, meaning "my people," and Lo-Ruhama becomes Ruhama, meaning "mercy." Hosea envisions God bringing them back to his good graces: "Behold, I will allure her and I will bring her to the desert and I will speak to her heart. I will give her a vineyard from there and the valley of Achor [trouble] as a door of hope, and she will respond there as in the days of her youth and as the day she went up from Egypt. It shall be on that day, says the Lord, she will call me Ishi [my husband] and not Baali [my master]" (2:14-16).

God and Israel will remember the covenants they formed when God brought the Israelites out of Egypt into the desert with great love, making them his special nation. Now God promises: "I shall betroth you to me forever, and I shall betroth you to me in righteousness and in justice and in kindness and in compassion, and I shall betroth you to me with faithfulness, and you shall know God" (2:19-20). This new betrothal will be loving, complete, and everlasting, and the bride (Israel) will know her husband (God) more closely than ever before.

IN THIS UNUSUAL but important story, the Israelites have begun to see God as one of the Baals. Instead of loving God and recognizing the blessings and love that are part of his covenant with them, they have come to see him as a power that needs to be pacified in order for them to receive his rewards. They see the bounty of the fields and deify nature. God realizes that the best way to teach Hosea is through the example and experience of the marriage vows. People can stray from the promises they have made and the covenant they have agreed to, as did Gomer, but this does not mean that there is no goodness or loyalty in them. This is what Hosea will feel toward Gomer — and God toward the Israelites. Hosea learns to love her despite her waywardness and despite his doubts.

God's doubt is reflected in the names of Hosea and Gomer's three children; but as the family goes on, God changes the names and accepts the family. The point of this story is that a person must grow from experience. People can find themselves in very strange situations, involved with or even married to someone they cannot fully trust; for example, it would be unrealistic for Hosea to totally forget Gomer's unsavory background. But his acceptance offers her a security and opportunity to change her ways. As a metaphor for God's relationship with his people, Hosea's marriage to Gomer is a shining example that the God of the covenant can always redeem those who have gone astray.

The Concubine at Gibeah (Judges 19–21)

The story of the concubine at Gibeah both begins and ends with the Bible declaring that "in those days there was no king in Israel," and then concludes with the statement that, because of that absence, "everyone did what was right in his own eyes." When a society begins to collapse, all kinds of horrors threaten. In this case, a man of the Levites takes as his concubine a woman from the town of Bethlehem. Concubinage was common enough in the ancient world, especially in nations where polygamy was legal: it is best described as a partial marriage that had fewer legal obligations between the two people than the usual marriage. The differences largely concerned matters of money and property. Apparently, the Levite and his concubine have quarreled, and she has returned to her father's home. As time passes, the husband grows lonesome and goes to Bethlehem to retrieve his concubine. Their reunion is pleasant, and after a visit of several days, they set out on the road back to their home in Mount Ephraim. Starting out later than they had planned, they are still on the road as the sun sets. They turn away from the Canaanite town of Jebus, fearful of mistreatment, and they go instead to the Israelite town of Gibeah. But no one offers hospitality until finally an elderly man, not a longtime resident, invites them to his home.

What follows is horrifying. A group of men surround the house so that no one can escape and demand that the Levite husband be surrendered to them for homosexual gang rape. The old man who is hosting the Levite and his concubine offers the mob his virgin daughter and the concubine instead — so that the men outside will not "act so wickedly," "commit this outrage," "do such a vile thing" (Judg. 19:23-24), that is, commit homosexual rape against the Levite. The Levite finally pushes his concubine outside and locks the door behind her. The men in the mob rape her until daybreak, and then they leave her at the front door of the house. In the morning, the husband opens the door and finds her dead.

This terrible crime provokes a massive reaction. Eleven Israelite tribes arm themselves to punish the tribe of Benjamin, to which

Gibeah belongs. Three bloody battles leave the tribe of Benjamin nearly annihilated, and many thousands are slain among the victorious eleven tribes of Israel as well.

It is only after the massive destruction of this civil war that peace is finally restored. The rape of the concubine is a dreadful act of uncontrolled hooligans, but the reaction to it is no better. The small group of criminals alone should have been severely punished. The massive civil war is the result of thoughtless anger, not the reasoned reply of a responsible government. Without wise and strong leadership, people will act as their will moves them for good or bad, not according to what is just or right or in accordance with God's will. An incident that could have been prevented exploded into a bloody destruction that likewise should never have happened. The need for a strong leader was clear, and it was not many years after this battle at Gibeah that Israel would have its first king. Saul came from this very same dissident tribe of Benjamin, and by some accounts he was one of their few survivors of the civil war.

THE CENTRAL CHARACTER in this story is a woman. Yet she plays only a small active role, and she dies miserably. Indeed, an active feminine voice is completely absent in this story. The reasons that the concubine has left her husband in the first place are unclear, but she may have sensed his lack of responsiveness to her. This absence of his care for her certainly shows itself in her terrible death: her husband sacrifices her to hooligans to save his own life. Second, no one appears to rectify the deed. Finally, almost the entire tribe of Benjamin (which has been estranged from the other eleven tribes of Israel) is annihilated in retaliation. What is missing in this story is the active voice of a woman and the strong wisdom often associated with women, qualities needed to restrain the response and direct it only against the guilty parties.

Someone was needed to convince the Israelite men that annihilating the entire tribe of Benjamin would only make things worse. The men show themselves to be too hotheaded and vengeful, and they do not consider the consequences of what they are doing. Men tend to settle quarrels with their fists, or with weapons, or by other violent means, while women often consider the complex consequences care-fully. We may speculate here that a woman such as Rebecca would have seen the need for calm on both sides; she would have recognized the real need to punish the malefactors but would have understood how devastating excessive vengefulness can be. In this story, a dreadful civil war over the violation of a woman could have been averted by the wisdom of a woman.

Cozbi (Numbers 24–25)

Perhaps the most dangerous challenge to the Israelites during their forty years in the Sinai desert was neither the error of the golden calf nor the wanton and vicious attack by the Amalekites, but the moral challenge at Shittim by the cult of Baal Peor. King Balak of Moab had hired Balaam, a Mesopotamian soothsayer, to curse the Israelites, but God instead made Balaam bless them. Blocked though he was, Balaam's pointless hatred of the Israelites did not diminish, and he gave the Moabites and their Midianite allies this powerful advice: these Israelites derive their strength from their moral loyalty to God; lure them into sin, and you will be able to defeat them. "And Israel abode in Shittim, and the people began to commit harlotry with the daughters of Moab" (Num. 25:1).

The worship of Baal Peor seems to have involved a total surrender to temple prostitution and disgusting anal rituals comparable to the Greek worship of Dionysus. Many Israelites had joined in the licen-tious rites being practiced by the followers of Baal Peor. In this story, God instructs Moses on how to handle the outbreak: the leaders need to be punished immediately and publicly. However, before Moses can begin to implement God's order, the crisis intensifies. Zimri, a prince of the tribe of Simeon, appears before Moses, bringing with him Cozbi, a beautiful Midianite princess. The name itself in Akkadian means "voluptuous" (it may well be that, rather than the name she was given at birth, this is a nickname deemed appropriate to her). With the woman Cozbi, Zimri is challenging Moses: Had not Moses himself married a woman of Midian? Why should Zimri be denied his pleasure with a Midianite? This effectively neutralizes Moses because, as he appears to be personally involved in the controversy, he can no longer be seen to function solely as the devoted emissary of God. He weeps in frustration.

Why did Cozbi and the Moabite and Midianite women agree to this role of seducing Israelite men into religious immorality, prostitution, and idolatry? It certainly appears that they were not unwilling; it may have been their way of giving of themselves to damage a hated enemy. The rituals of Peor were not strange and abhorrent to Cozbi and her countrymen, as they were to the Israelites, for such rituals were widespread in the ancient world. So it would appear that the Moabite and Midianite leaders deliberately hatched this plan to destroy the Israelites, and they did not hesitate to use their own daughters to carry it out. The Midrash even suggests that one part of the plan was for Cozbi, a princess, to seduce Moses himself, but that Zimri, as a prince of the Simeonites, persuaded her that he was no less important. Scripture goes on to tell how Phinehas took the matter into his own hands by killing Zimri and Cozbi *in flagrante delicto,* stopping the plague.

The trauma of Peor caused long-term damage. Twenty-four thousand Israelites died in the plague, compared to only three thousand after the golden calf fiasco. Decades later, Joshua mentioned the effects on his people. The tribe of Simeon seems to have in some measure lost its individual identity. Moses does not give the tribe an individual blessing (in Deuteronomy 32) as he does the other eleven tribes, and they do not seem to have taken their own individual portion of the land of Israel.

WHAT MAKES A WOMAN like Cozbi do this? Cozbi and the other women were probably willing servants of Baal and of what was perceived as the national interests of Moab and Midian. Cozbi does not seem stupid or incapable, and her skill in seduction may give her a sense of power and purpose that she is using in a negative way. Perhaps she is a kind of Mata Hari of her cult and her people. Perhaps she has felt excluded from God and thus can gain a sense of purpose by undermining the faith of those who believe in him. Yet, if such a woman's talent could have been focused in a constructive manner, she could have been a great moral force in her society; indeed, it is her very lack of good purpose that leads her to use her talents to waste and destroy.

And one may wonder why Zimri is so drawn to a woman like Cozbi. What makes her so seductive? Perhaps it is that she seems to offer the illusion of passion without restriction. Women like Cozbi project an allure that entraps a man in a way that many wives may not seem to offer. The seductive appeal of a Cozbi may be heightened if she takes the initiative with Zimri, thus relieving him of the sense of responsibility and restriction he should have. This is intoxicating in itself: it casts Zimri as a carrier of fate, which overcomes his loyalty to his people's ways. If Zimri had had the faith of a man like Joseph, he might have been strong enough to make a wiser decision. Intellect alone is not enough. Cozbi is a Dionysian force that overcomes any resistance that Zimri may show and plays on his weaknesses.

The Priest's Daughter (Leviticus 19, 21; Deuteronomy 23)

Sexuality is the process through which God ordained that people will and must propagate their own kind. When he blessed the first couple, God said, "Be fruitful and multiply and fill the earth." The Genesis account shows sexual intercourse between Adam and Eve and later couples to be healthy and necessary, indeed obligatory. This is the very first commandment that God gave to the newly created Adam and Eve. Sexuality is an important and unique part of the interaction and intimacy between husband and wife. The Genesis story is so simple and straightforward that it is surprising to learn how very different the attitudes of other ancient cultures were in these matters. Ancient myths are replete with stories of people — and indeed gods — who use and abuse each other sexually. Rape, deception, and falsehood are so common as to seem not only normal but even heroic and exciting.

Sexuality was often turned into a form of conquest and oppression, which typically expressed selfishness and dominance, not warmth, life, and creativity — as Genesis intended. Calling prostitution "the world's oldest profession" would seem to be a cynical joke, perhaps reflecting the fact that it has to a certain extent been glorified in modern Western society. With friendly and benign names such as "Sweet Charity," the "Happy Hooker," Madame Saigon, or the noble prostitute in *Never on Sunday,* a variety of courtesans, harlots, prostitutes, ladies of the evening, and so on have played roles in history, literature, music, and film, and they are sometimes glorified or even sanctified, such as Sonya in *Crime and Punishment.*

But the view of Scripture is that the temple prostitution so widespread in ancient Mesopotamia and among the Canaanites and Phoenicians is oppressive and evil. Women would typically be required by law to offer themselves to men in the local temple over a certain period of time, or for a set number of sexual encounters, sometimes associated with life-cycle events. These temples also included career prostitutes. There were probably a number of reasons for this practice. One of the most prominent was that ancient religions were deeply involved in fertility cults, and these practiced many kinds of specific and symbolic sexual rites. Some demanded a sexual act between a priestess and a high priest (representing either a god or himself) that was symbolically aimed at promoting the fertility of not only the people but also of the crops and herds. Temple prostitution could offer the appearance of breaking down inhibitions, and the prostitutes could also make money for the temple.

Prostitutes could be male as well as female. Many cults propounded the myth of a goddess who had an earthly lover, who was then either castrated or killed — sometimes by the goddess herself. Cybele, for example, was a major goddess in Asia Minor and later in Rome. Priests were typically eunuchs in some way effeminate, and these men would surrender their sexual identities totally to the power of the goddess. The ancients, like modern cultists, often did strange things in order to gain a sense of belonging to a group. All of these rites and activities involved a debasement of character and individuality that is antithetical to the Bible's great love of humankind and to its many rules to prevent the denigration or desecration of the human body. And the rites also meant a surrender of one's sexual identity that is again wholly opposed by the Bible.

Sexual activity between two partners sanctified to each other in marriage reflects both human creativity and closeness to God. But prostitution of the non-sacred sort is a debasing of healthy creative sexuality and of the relationship between God and humanity. Paganism sensed the power of the sex drive, but it did not develop the relationship in a healthy perspective of holiness. A man and woman who function sexually within the holiness and modesty of the marriage bond keep open the lines of communication with God. They have a sense of the importance of their relationship and of what they can create, and they enjoy living together. Neither sees the other as merely an object to use.

A further issue is the use of sex to satisfy one's own sordid greed and sense of power. A father who sells his daughter and a woman who sells herself are debasing both their persons and the great gifts of humanity and creativity that God has given them. The uniqueness of human sexual intimacy is at the basis of the family structure. Deuteronomy 23:18-19 specifically commands that there shall be no prostitute, male or female, among the people of Israel. Nor is a prostitute allowed to donate her wages to the Temple, for social and sexual depravity could not be associated with the sacred. Leviticus 19:29 adds that a father must not profane his daughter by giving her over for prostitution. The laws restricting illicit sexuality apply to both men and women, because illicit sex leads to the destruction of family life. People will lose a healthy sense of identity and purpose.

The priest is held to a higher standard of sexual purity than is a non-priest, and a high priest to the strictest of all. The latter may marry only a virgin (Lev. 21:13). One reason is that a wife of a high priest in essence shares in his elevated sanctity, and it is preferable that she be a person who has never experienced even in thought a strong sexual attraction to any man besides her husband. Also a priest's daughter who commits adultery is punished with a harsher death penalty than a non-priest's daughter for the same sin (Lev. 21:9).

SOMETIMES PEOPLE find themselves coerced into sexual or marital situations that are inherently degrading, for example, prostitution or entering a marriage for financial reasons. Esther was forcibly conscripted into the harem of Ahasuerus. Yet she did not become embittered or corrupted, nor did she forget that she was a daughter of Israel. With the help of her uncle, Mordecai, she used her position to carry out the divine purpose of saving the Israelites from Haman's evil plot. She made the best of what could have been a very destructive situation. What happened to her was affected by her own faith and by the support of people close to her, and also by the willingness of Ahasueros to see the quality of her personality.

A woman who has been raped has been violated through no fault of her own; yet she is held to be guilty and responsible in many cultures. This rejection by those around her can be more damaging than the original rape: not believing her becomes something like a second rape. But also, in a non-forced situation, a woman may freely enter a marriage but may become a participant in turning that marriage into something like prostitution — by using her sexuality to extract gifts or financial reward from her husband rather than engaging in sex as an expression of love.

Conjugal Rights

Human sexuality has become a complicated and much misunderstood motif of Western society, as we are continually reminded at drugstore magazine racks and in Hollywood movies. The Bible's view is much more straightforward. In the very first chapter of Genesis, God's first command to the newly created Adam and Eve is to "be fruitful and multiply." The two went unclothed in the Garden of Eden without feeling ashamed of their bodies; indeed, it had never been suggested to them that nakedness or sexuality was evil. In fact, sexuality is not only a blessing but also a command. Later, Scripture sets out many laws and practices to safeguard the sanctity of sex and to protect the strength and purity of families. A person who lives by the biblical norms can regulate and change his or her sexual drive in healthy ways, ways that respect herself or himself and others. Such a person will not see himself or herself as subject to the arrows of Cupid or the whims of Aphrodite: sex is not a matter of conquest or surrender.

The Lysistrata, a classic Greek comedy by Aristophanes, focuses on the theme that the women of Greece have organized a sex strike to force their men to stop fighting the Peloponnesian War, a theme that lends itself to overt bawdy and bodily jokes, as well as political satire. The Lysistrata operates with a rather cavalier notion of sex that contrasts with the Bible's view of sex as blessing and command. Indeed, Exodus 21 lists sex among the duties that a husband owes his wife: "her food, her clothing, and her conjugal rights he shall not diminish" (21:10). Later commentators suggest that even some amount of simple bodily closeness is also required. Sex is not used in the Bible to reward or punish, in contrast to Plato's suggestion for the citizens of his utopian republic. It is an expression of human creativity at its most personal level by which a husband and wife enhance their own intimacy and produce new human beings.

BOTH WOMEN AND MEN can use sex in either destructive or constructive ways. Women and men need each other for both sexual fulfillment and reproduction. If either aspect is ignored, the sexuality is incomplete. A generation of sexologists in America was captured by Alfred Kinsey's assertion that American women did not reach orgasm. What was missing in Kinsey's formulation was the role of intimacy and bonding. People can reach physical orgasm without a partner. Sex with a partner involves the bonding and fulfillment of a relationship and is essential to God's plan for reproduction of the human race. Being a powerful force, sex can be used destructively or for manipulation, as it was in The Lysistrata. Manipulative withdrawal to get one's way (more typical of women) or, at the other extreme, coercive sex (more typical of men) can occur within marriage as well as outside it.

CHAPTER 7

Women as Daughters

A reader of classic Athenian plays such as *Antigone, Iphigenia at Aulis,* and *Electra* will be amazed at their grandeur yet at the same time appalled by the profoundly dysfunctional relationships between parents and daughters. For they use each other rather than loving each other, and they seek to create bonds that stifle growth and pay no regard to the natural human urge toward self-fulfillment. The Bible offers a number of stories that point in a new direction. Daughters can grow into independent and healthy adults who respect their parents and are attached to them without being enmeshed with them. Achsa and the daughters of Zelophehad exemplify this pattern. The mutual support that Naomi and Ruth give each other — even though they were actually mother-in-law and daughter-in-law, they became like mother and daughter — provides a remarkable account of unjealous giving and love. The laws concerning the Hebrew maidservant offer some regulation of the father-daughter interaction, which moves in a very different direction from the Greek father-daughter relationship. Even so, the tragic story of Jephthah's daughter portrays the horrible outcome of an unsolicited vow foolishly made — and even more foolishly kept.

But the Bible is never hesitant to tell the truth about its characters: it never whitewashes even its most notable figures, teaching us the honest lessons that we need to learn from their all-too-human flaws and failures. Therefore, this chapter provides accounts of Lot's daughters, and also of Michal, the brilliant but turbulent daughter of one king and the wife of his successor.

Achsa (Joshua 15:16-19; Judges 2)

The story of Achsa takes only four verses for the Bible to tell, yet it is told twice — once in Joshua 15 and then again in Judges 2. As the forty years in the Sinai were coming to an end, Moses divided up the land of Israel among the Israelite people. He gave the city of Hebron and the surrounding area to Caleb, a distinguished man who had acted heroically in the incident of the twelve spies (Numbers 13). Now well on in years but still valiant, Caleb drives out the powerful Anakim in this story and takes possession of Hebron. Going up next against Kiryat Sefer, Caleb offers his beautiful daughter in marriage to whoever will move out and capture it; so Othniel, apparently the son of Caleb's younger half-brother, takes the city and gains Achsa's hand.

The next part of the story is difficult to interpret, but it offers a deep psychological message. Joshua 15:18 says: "And it was when she came to him [Othniel], she persuaded him to ask her father for a field." She dismounts from her donkey and approaches her father, and Caleb says to her, literally, "What is wanting to you?" Achsah goes on to explain that the land Caleb has given the newlyweds has no water supply. Caleb responds by giving her and her husband the "upper and lower springs."

What is so important about this brief episode that Scripture sees the need to tell it twice, or indeed to tell it at all? And why is it necessary to narrate details such as Achsa riding a donkey, then dismounting from it, to meet with her father? The sages of the Talmud offer a unique view of the story. The Talmud says that Achsa was so great a beauty that men who looked at her became angry at their own wives, punning on the name Achsa and its similarity to the word *caasa*, which means angry. Achsa perhaps rode the donkey to indicate that, just as a donkey brays when it needs something, so Achsa needed something from her father. Her message to Caleb is that, though her husband is a noted warrior and a great scholar, he isn't necessarily a wage earner, and their house is lacking in certain material necessities.

Achsa's pressing her cause with her father shows a practical wisdom and benevolence. Rather than belittling Othniel for not being what he is not, she turns for material help to Caleb. Apparently, by arriving alone and using the donkey as a symbol, Achsa is able to make her point clearly and to get what she needs without damaging these three important relationships — between herself and her husband, between herself and her father, and between her husband and her father. Othniel will go on to become a national hero by leading his people's forces to victory against the invading forces of King Cushan Rishatayim.

TWO THINGS ARE STRIKING in this story. First, Othniel is a warrior as well as a scholar; second, Caleb seems unaware of his nephew's personality. The donkey's bray can be very persistent, demanding attention. Perhaps Achsa feels she needs to remind Caleb of something he already knows, but her way of bringing the problem to her father's attention shows a sensitivity typical of great biblical women toward their menfolk. A woman, through her sensitivity and intuition, can know a man's strengths and weaknesses inside and out. The issue is how she uses this knowledge. By brutally criticizing a man, a woman can destroy his self-confidence and leave him feeling impotent — both physically and psychologically — and thus she becomes his greatest enemy. Or she can function as a helpmeet-opposite, recognizing and compensating for his limitations and complementing his strengths.

Achsa is just such a helpmeet. She does not expect from Othniel what he cannot do, but she treasures him for what he can do. She is able to ask for her father's help without damaging Othniel's sense of self-worth. The way she approaches Caleb also shows her sensitivity and respect as a daughter. She understands that he may have ignored certain matters. Rather than confront him directly, she uses the donkey to awaken Caleb to her needs. Yet she dismounts from the donkey to show respect toward her father, enabling Caleb to feel that he has acted on his own.

Zelophehad's Daughters (Numbers 27)

It seems that women often have less difficulty than men in adjusting to changing conditions, and the story of the five daughters of Zelophehad represents such a case. Near the end of their forty years in the Sinai, the Israelites have been deeply traumatized by their bitter experience at Peor. Midianite women enticed Israelite men into the orgiastic rituals of the local Baal cult, and God's anger about this transgressing has caused him to send a plague among the people that has killed 24,000 Israelites.

The significance of both the sin and the plague is so telling that it can be felt for many years to come. At this moment of Israel's failure of moral will, it is the women who emerge to give strength to the nation. In this narrative in Numbers 27, five women of the tribe of Manasseh come forward to claim a share in the division of the land of Israel. Their father, Zelophehad, has died and has left behind these five daughters, but no sons. Should his share of the land be lost and his name forgotten in Israel, they ask, simply because he had no sons? Or should his daughters inherit his assigned lands (Num. 27:1-4)?

The sisters, all unmarried, step forward before Moses and the leaders of Israel and express in their petition a faith and commitment to the future of the land of Israel that many men have been willing to throw away in an orgy only a little while before — just as it has been the women and not the men who have stayed loyal and strong through the crises of the golden calf and the spies.

The daughters of Zelophehad are wise and devoted women who are following their ancestors Joseph and Jacob in their love of the land of Israel. Both these men had expressed their strong desire to be buried in Israel rather than in Egypt. Now the women want to do their best both to help in settling the new land and in honoring their father. They point out that Zelophehad has been no enemy either of Moses or of the ways of Israel; he has not been part of the rebellion of Korah, but has died "in his own sin" (27:3).

Moses does not wish to decide the case on his own, or perhaps he cannot. He tells the women that he will consult with God. Again it seems that the women are thinking more clearly than the wise leader. And God's decision is not only in favor of the women but complimentary to them: "The daughters of Zelophehad speak correctly. Give them their father's share of the land among his brethren." Then God goes on to explain some additional laws of inheritance (27:6-12). The Midrash adds that God also tells Moses that the women's plea is quite in line with his own law. "Thus is the chapter written before me in heaven." In their wisdom, the daughters of Zelophehad have understood what Moses himself has not.

THIS STORY DRAMATICALLY PORTRAYS the critical role of women in maintaining the purpose of a society through devastating times — times when individual and group needs can be trampled and dismissed. The five daughters of Zelophehad know a better way. They seek their land as an expression not merely of acquisitiveness but of the purposes of the God of Israel and in their unshakable belief that God keeps his promises. In this story they are portrayed as wiser in this matter than Moses himself. God knows that the search of these women for their rights arises from a deep sense of his covenant with Israel. The women are not acting in ways that are oppositional to the law and the covenant, refusing to cooperate out of petty spite or hunger for power; but they are acting from a deep realization that God cares about what might be regarded as small events in people's lives. For no event in a person's life, however small it might seem, is unimportant to God, the Creator of the universe. How different this is from the relative lack of interest among the many gods of paganism to issues of ethics and morality.

Nor are the biblical women separated from moral issues, as in the Freudian scheme that views women as having less developed superegos. So often in Scripture, when things seem to be falling apart, it is women who are able to put them back together.

Lot's Daughters (Genesis 19)

Ovid, the great Roman poet, recounts the myth of Myrrha, who was smitten by the goddess Aphrodite with a fierce passion for her father, Cyneras. The goddess wanted to punish Cyneras for not paying suitable deference to her. Myrrha comes to her father without his recognizing her, either because it is dark or because he is drunk. The incestuous rendezvous continues for twelve nights, until Cyneras discovers who his lover has been. Disgusted, he tries to kill her, but she runs away and is finally turned into a tree — the tree that produces myrrh, which was used in perfume and incense. The son of Cyneras and Myrrha is Adonis, who becomes a lover of Aphrodite. This story is typical of Greek myths: the gods compel a person into a miserable situation that leads to his or her great harm or even destruction.

The Bible also tells a story of a father-daughter sexual encounter; however, the circumstances and the characters are very unlike the Greek story of Myrrha. Abraham's nephew Lot has settled in the city of Sodom, which is so wicked that God has decided to destroy the city utterly; but he sends angels in the form of men to warn Lot to lead his family out. The angels enter the city, and Lot invites them to accept his hospitality. Hospitality is the practice of Abraham's household, but the Sodomites see it as a criminal act that threatens their own security and wealth.

A menacing mob gathers in front of Lot's house demanding that the visitors come out — "that we may know them." They may have simply wanted to see if the visitors were worth robbing or doing business with; but the phrase may also suggest homosexual rape. Coming outside to calm the mob, Lot urges them not to behave badly and even offers them his two daughters for their sport, if they will leave the guests unharmed: "Here now are my two daughters whom no man has known. I will bring them out to you, and you may do to them what is good in your eyes. Only to these men do no wrong, because for this they have come under the protection of my roof" (19:8).

The mob grows more agitated and moves forward to break down the door. At this point, the angels pull Lot inside to safety and strike the attackers with some manner of confusion or blindness so that, despite their continuing efforts, they cannot find the door. Lot's behavior seems horrifying. A normal healthy man would give his life to protect his family, not hand them over to a mob. It may be that Lot is merely trying to divert the mob and cool them down, and he would never have actually given the daughters to them. Yet one wonders, especially in the light of subsequent events, whether his answer shows a lack of feeling for the daughters or some need to debase them.

Lot's approach to his sons-in-law is also noteworthy. He tries to persuade them to flee Sodom with him, but they merely laugh at him. The married daughters are not mentioned: perhaps they are left out of the discussion, or perhaps they side with their husbands. In either case, it seems that Lot does not exercise enough influence on them to induce them to flee. After failing to convince his married daughters and their husbands to join the escape, Lot and his wife and the two single daughters flee at dawn. Lot's wife, of course, never makes it out, because she turns into a pillar of salt when she looks back at the exploding city. But Lot and the two daughters reach the small town of Zoar, and from there they flee to a cave in the hills. Perhaps they stop in Zoar only because Lot is no longer a youngster and does not have the strength to journey farther that day.

In the cave the elder daughter offers her sister a strange suggestion: "Our father is old, and there is no man on the earth to come on us in the way of all the earth. Come, let us ply our father with wine and let us lie with him, and let us produce children from our father." The daughters carry out their plan. On successive nights they get Lot drunk so that he will drop his guard and his inhibitions and have intercourse with them. Either he is totally unaware of their coming in to him or he is enough affected by the wine not to resist. But in the end both young women become pregnant and give birth to sons, and these two sons become the eponymous ancestors of the nations of Moab and Ammon.

Why do these young women take on so desperate a plan? Perhaps they think that all mankind has been destroyed in the destruction of Sodom and that this is the only way to continue the human race. If so, their plan is at least in one sense positive — even if it is very wrong. They apparently do believe that their region has been destroyed and that there are no other remaining men nearby with whom they can have children.

Lot himself is certainly a man who can at times put his own desires ahead of his moral obligations. He has separated from Abraham and his spiritual way of life in order to settle in the wealthy but depraved city of Sodom. Whatever Lot may have been thinking when he offered his daughters for the pleasure of the Sodomite mob, the daughters must have been terrified and humiliated. And why was that the strategy that came to Lot's mind in a moment of crisis? He may have had an attachment to lewdness, and he certainly was insensitive to the well-being of his daughters and to their feelings, and may have been to women in general. Perhaps Lot is now an easy mark for his daughters' plot because he does not resist getting drunk and indulging in gratifying his sexual needs with the nearest females. There may even be something of a revenge motive in his older daughter's naming of her child: she names her infant son Moab (meaning "from my father"), thus announcing to whoever is left in the world that she has conceived this boy by her father, that the child is simultaneously Lot's son and grandson.

THIS STORY HIGHLIGHTS an evil and destructive mixture of separation and attachment between father and daughter. Lot's two married daughters show insufficient attachment to him, and he to them. While it is true that women, once they are married, should be loyal to their husbands rather than their parents, they must also assert themselves as opposites when necessary. When Lot warns his two married daughters of the danger to them and to their families, they should not have remained foolishly silent in the wake of their husbands' obtuseness. They should have spoken up: this would not have made them less loyal to their husbands, but more loyal.

Lot's two unmarried daughters, the ones who flee Sodom with him, prove to be insufficiently separated from their father, as he is from them. When Lot offers those two daughters to the bullies in

Sodom, he is treating them as objects of barter. And when these two get him drunk so that he can impregnate them without being conscious of the guilt of incest, they are treating him as an object — just as he treated them. Lot and his daughters treat each other as extensions of themselves, using each other for their own purposes; each sees the other as an agent or instrument to fulfill personal need.

Neither set of Lot's daughters displays the integration of individuation and attachment that is the hallmark of the healthy biblical helpmeet-opposite, and thus both sets of relationships are unsuccessful.

Jephthah's Daughter (Judges 11)

Jephthah's daughter is never named either in the Bible or in the supporting oral traditions, yet she stands out as one of the saddest of figures. At some point during the era of the Judges, the Israelites were being sorely harassed by the neighboring Midianites. In this story in Judges 11, the Israelite elders call on Jephthah to help them. Jephthah is a son of Gilead, born not to his principal wife but to a concubine or possibly a prostitute. Jephthah's fully legitimate brothers have refused to include him in their inheritance and have driven him away to the land of Tov, where he becomes head of an outlaw band. But now Jephthah accepts the Israelite elders' offer and leads the Israelites to victory against their enemies. Before going into battle, he makes a vow to God that, whatever he sees first when he returns home victorious, he will offer as a sacrifice — a most unthinking vow (Judg. 11:30-31).

When Jephthah does return from his glorious victory, it is his daughter, his only child, who comes out to greet him with joy and music. Jephthah, in despair, tells her of his oath and the fact that he cannot back down from it now that God has given him victory. Later writers have commented that, under the circumstances, Jephthah should have gone to the high priest and had his vow annulled. However, Jephthah does no such thing; either he truly feels that his vow should stand, or he feels that it would be demeaning to ask the priest for favors. The poor girl is lost. She acquiesces to her situation without complaint, asking only for two months to go up to the mountains and meditate on her condition.

The first being to emerge from Jephthah's house upon his return could have been a donkey or a cat, both unfit for sacrifice by biblical law. Indeed, Jephthah did not stop to think that there could be no more suitable welcome for a victorious general than the women of his household coming to hail him with rejoicing and songs and dancing. One medieval Midrash says that Jephthah was familiar with the idolatrous rites of the neighboring Canaanites, who worshiped their Baals in the form of child sacrifice, and that he intended to sacrifice his daughter to his own god.

Scripture goes on to relate that Jephthah carries out his vow, though the specifics are unclear. Some scholars think that he actually sacrificed her himself. Others argue that she lived a solitary and celibate life in the mountains, devoted to prayer and religious thought. Jephthah was shortsighted as well: this daughter was his only child, so he was canceling his own future as he was fulfilling his ill-conceived oath. (The Talmud labels Jephthah as the least qualified of the leaders of Israel in the premonarchic times.)

MAKING A VOW can be a complicated act; sometimes it is made under duress or in extenuating circumstances, and in such cases should not be kept. During the period after the Russian Revolution, coauthor Kalman Kaplan's maternal grandmother, Kraina Saposnik, was leading her children through the woods near Chernobyl to escape a pogrom against Jews. They were suddenly stopped by a group of gangsters who were going to kill them. Though short in stature, Kraina was very quick-witted. She recognized the leader of this gang as a man named Shtruk; she had applied ground-up herbs to his sores when he was a child. Kraina knew that Shtruk came from a Christian family, and she introduced herself to him, crying out in desperation: "Do you think your God will not see what you are doing?"

Shtruk remembered her from his childhood, and he did not really want to kill her and her children. But he was afraid that she would turn him and his gang in to the authorities. He asked for assurance that she would not do so. Kraina made a vow to him that she would not, and she sealed that vow with the Ukrainian custom of swallowing a piece of earth. Shtruk relented and let Kraina and her children go on their way.

When the little family came to Chernobyl, Kraina told her children that she had to break her vow in the interest of saving the lives of other people whom Shtruk and his gang might stop in the woods. So she immediately reported the gang's whereabouts to the authorities in the town. The gang was captured the next day, and they were all hanged in the public square of Chernobyl. Kraina felt that she had to break her vow to save other lives.

WHY DID JEPHTHAH'S DAUGHTER accept her father's oath with no argument or discussion? Probably she knew little more of Israelite law than her father did, and she may not have realized that human sacrifice was altogether forbidden and that vows could be annulled by the proper authorities. Perhaps she felt that refusing to go along with her father's vow would demean his heroism at an important moment of national history.

But there may have been another reason for Jephthah's daughter's action. She may have gone along not because she thought he was right but because she thought this was part of a divine plan that would reveal itself in the same way that Abraham's binding of Isaac revealed itself: God would send an angel to prevent the sacrifice in the same way that he did for Isaac. But God did not order Jephthah to stay his hand, because God had not ordered the sacrifice in the first place. The only chance she felt she had to stop her father's action was to find a way that would not humiliate him. How could she do it? Perhaps she thought that her two months of going off to the mountains would give him a chance to change his course. But he did not change his course. She herself left no children, and Jephthah suffered the loss of the possibility of any progeny.

Michal (I Samuel 18; II Samuel 3:13-16; 6:16, 23)

Michal, the daughter of King Saul and wife of King David, is an enigmatic figure. She is first mentioned in I Samuel 14:49 as the younger sister of Merab; she is not mentioned again until I Samuel 18:20: "Michal, the daughter of Saul, loved David." Learning that Michal has fallen in love with David, Saul is pleased (18:21), and he offers her to David in marriage after Merab marries someone else. However, Saul is not simply behaving like a happy father, nor is David necessarily behaving like a happy bridegroom. The story is more complex than that — for several reasons.

First, while the text describes Michal's love for David, it does not mention David's feelings toward Michal. Second, earlier in the book of I Samuel, a "man of Israel" has said that "the man who strikes [Goliath] down, the king will enrich him with a great fortune, and his daughter he will give him" (I Sam. 17:25). King Saul initially supports the young shepherd David after his amazing conquest of the Philistine giant Goliath; but he soon begins to be apprehensive of David's success and the people's adulation of him. First, Saul wishes to give his elder daughter, Merab, to David in marriage because of his success in fighting the Philistines: "Her shall I give you as a wife, only be a valiant fellow for me and fight the battles of the Lord" (18:17). He says that aloud, but what he is thinking is: "Let not my hand be against him, but let the hand of the Philistines be against him" (18:17). But David demurs, saying that his humble origins and family background do not qualify him to be the son-in-law of the king.

So King Saul gives his daughter Merab to another man in marriage. But when Saul learns that his younger daughter, Michal, secretly loves David, he is pleased because he believes that Michal will be "a snare to him, and that the hand of the Philistines may be against him" (18:21). One way or the other, Saul is clearly hoping that David will die in one of his encounters with the Philistines. Once again he offers David, through the word of mouth of his servants and messengers, the privilege of becoming his son-in-law. But David demurs again, saying that he does not deserve to be the king's son-in-law because he is "a poor and lightly esteemed man" — although he has been greeted with the song and dance of the women of Israel. King Saul replies — again through intermediaries — that he does not require any dowry from David; the only requirement is for him to slay one hundred Philistines as Saul's vengeance on them and bring back their foreskins to Saul (18:25).

When David comes back from that expedition successfully, he now clearly desires to become the king's son-in-law (18:26-27), and Saul gives David his daughter Michal as his wife. But Saul is increasingly anxious and unhappy about David's abilities and popularity, and he clearly hopes that either David will be killed in battle or that Michal will serve as her father's spy in David's household. However, Michal proves to be anything but docile and cooperative. On one occasion, when Saul sends soldiers to seize David in his house so that they can kill him, Michal helps David escape through a window. She then places a dummy of David in his bed, with his clothes on and goats' hair as fake hair for him; she delays Saul's agents on the pretext that David is sick. Later, in response to Saul's accusations that she has deceived him, she lies to her father again, saying that David threatened to kill her if she did not help him escape (19:11-17).

David escapes from Saul more than once in the ensuing chapters of I Samuel, but the next time we hear about Michal is in a single sentence in I Samuel 25:44, which says that, although she is already married to David, "Saul had given Michal his daughter, David's wife, to Palti ben Laish." Prior to this, the text tells us that by this time David has taken both Abigail and Ahinoam as wives (25:42-43). And we do not encounter Michal again for some time.

After Saul's death, rivalry between the house of Saul and the house of David goes on for a long time, and David grows stronger while the house of Saul becomes weaker. During this period Abner, Saul's most prominent general, becomes incensed because of an accusation against him by Saul's son Ish-bosheth, and he decides to transfer his loyalty to David (II Sam. 3:6-12), and thus, as he puts it, "transfer the kingdom from the house of Saul, and set up the throne of David over Israel" (3:10). David agrees to make a covenant with Abner, but he insists that Abner bring his wife Michal back to him. Abner simply takes her from

Palti ben Laish and returns her to David (3:15). Palti accompanies them, weeping all the way, as far as Bahurim, where Abner orders him to go back home (3:16). We know nothing of Michal's feelings about all this and indeed do not hear from her again for a good while. We learn about King Saul's death in a battle with the Philistines in a description that closes the book of I Samuel (I Samuel 31).

Years pass, and David becomes king of all Israel; he also takes other concubines and wives (II Samuel 5). The Holy Ark of the Tabernacle, which had been captured by the Philistines after various mishaps, David now brings to Jerusalem, an event the people celebrate with a magnificent procession, many sacrifices and offerings, dancing, and great rejoicing. David himself, clad in a priest's tunic, leads the procession and dances joyously with all his might, filled with the love of God. But Michal mysteriously appears once again, watching from a window of the royal residence, and she is not happy: "She despise[s] him in her heart" for what seems to her to be David's lack of royal dignity (II Sam. 6:16). David completes the ceremonies, blesses the people in God's name, distributes gifts of food to all the assembled people, and sends them on their way. He then returns to his own home to give a blessing on it; but before he enters the door, Michal comes out and assails him with a torrent of sarcasm: "How honored today was the king of Israel, who showed himself off before the maidservants of his servants, just as the low class people are seen."

As Robert Alter points out in his book *The David Story*,[1] Michal addresses David in the third person, and in a most sarcastic manner. David responds to her bluntly, asserting his own royal credentials and telling Michal that he will do whatever he must — and furthermore that the maidservants do indeed respect him: "I rejoiced before the Lord, who chose me over your father and all his house to be ruler over the people of God, over Israel. And I will humble myself indeed more than this, and I will be lowly in my own eyes, and with the maidservants of whom you speak I shall be honored" (6:21-22). On the one hand, David seems moved by a higher purpose. David tells Michal that

---

1. Robert Alter, *The David Story* (New York: W. W. Norton, 1999), pp. 228-29.

he has been raised to the throne at God's command, not by popular election, and the purpose of his rule is to dedicate himself totally to serving God. He does not have to demonstrate his royal status to the masses; instead, he intends to lead them in serving God.

On the other hand, David may be feeling like an insulted husband — thus his sharp reaction to Michal's attack on him. We have noted that the text gives us nothing concerning David's feelings toward Michal. He may have loved her but lost hope of ever having her back after Saul took her back and gave her in marriage to Palti ben Laish (which is very curious indeed, and in violation of Jewish law). Polygyny was legal during this period of Israel's history, so David's taking of other wives does not necessarily imply that he no longer wants Michal. When General Abner changes loyalties, and David insists that the latter return Michal to him, does he do so for Machiavellian reasons — that is, at least partly to show that he has gained the upper hand over Saul — or because he still loves her? David's angry response to Michal's sarcasm may be motivated by the pain he feels in her reaction to him, which would show that he still loves her.

In any case, the story of Michal ends on a sad note, suggesting that the love Michal once had for David has disappeared, and that David himself wants nothing more to do with her. "And Michal, daughter of Saul, had no child till her dying day" (6:23).

THE CRITICAL QUESTION at the end of this story is why Michal speaks so harshly to David when she sees him celebrating with the multitudes when the ark of the covenant is brought to Jerusalem. Do her words indicate a change in her attitude toward David, a man she once loved? Do they reflect a certain haughtiness in her character? There is much in the story to suggest the first alternative. Michal is often treated as an object. She is Saul's daughter, but in what sense can Saul be described as Michal's father? First, he intends to marry David to his older daughter Merab, with the intention of ensnaring him. He switches to Michal when he discovers that she loves David, but again, his aim is to use her to ensnare David. After David flees, Saul gives Michal to Palti ben Laish.

Saul acts toward Michal out of motives that always set his interests above hers. Even though Michal saves David's life and then lies to her father, David continues to take other wives and concubines, which was not unusual in this period. When David becomes king, he demands that Michal be returned to him. Perhaps Michal's anger toward David finally erupts when she sees David celebrating with the multitudes.

On the other hand, Michal's speech may indicate a type of haughtiness that is genuinely embarrassed by David's common touch. Commentators offer two quite different insights supporting this interpretation. In one view, she was saying to David that her father had ruled with royal dignity, always dressing and behaving every inch a king. How could David lower himself to dance in public in so undignified a manner? In this view, Michal, princess of a royal line, is embarrassed by David's behavior.

A second midrash notes that Michal is once referred to in the book of Samuel by the name Eglah, meaning "young heifer," which would indicate Michal's fierce need for independence. She has often disagreed with Saul and rebelled against restriction, just as the young heifer struggles against the yoke. In this view, Michal may well have been disturbed by the several instances when her father has given in to the desires of his subjects — even in disobedience to divine command. In these matters Saul insisted too little on his royal dignity, and it hurt his kingship beyond repair. In this view, Michal loves David very much, and now she sees him leaping and dancing like the common people would, and this disgusts her precisely because it seems like the same mistake her father made. The two instances when her father entered into a prophetic trance and went naked in public may have been particularly galling to her. If David has no sense of royal dignity, she feels, his rule likewise will crumble. In fact, these two views are not necessarily in contradiction: Michal may well feel a certain ambivalence toward both her father and her husband.

But Michal is mistaken in equating David's behavior with that of Saul. Saul's going naked in public may have represented a weakening of his inner self-definition, but David's behavior is different: he shows his love of God and his attachment to his people, not as a diminishing of his own being but as its fulfillment. Michal's failure to distinguish between these two motivations leads her to put Saul's face on David. Although Michal has acted as a helpmeet-opposite to David in saving his life earlier in the story, her behavior at the end of the story seems designed to humiliate him and hurt him to the core. This is behavior that is typical of Greek heroines, not biblical women. It is difficult to decide whether Michal's behavior is due to the callous treatment she has received from her father (and perhaps from David as well), or whether it reflects a haughtiness and inability to engage as a full partner.

The Hebrew Maidservant (Exodus 21:7-11)

The ancient Roman law gave the father, or *paterfamilias,* great power over the members of his household. He was authorized to sell his children, sons or daughters, as slaves, and he could even execute them. Children were hardly less threatened in Phoenicia, where they could be offered as human sacrifice; archaeologists have found extensive remains of these horrifying rites. Throughout Greece, parents could expose a newborn child to death, and specifically in Sparta, where newborns who appeared unfit to grow up to be soldiers were thrown to their deaths off Mount Taygetus. Slaves in these societies of the ancient world were nothing but property and could be tortured, killed, or castrated. Only in late antiquity did pagan society begin to show any interest in their welfare.

The Bible set up the laws of the "Hebrew maidservant," which seem at first glance to parallel the pagans' rules about daughters but are, in fact, very different. Exodus 21:7-11 declares that a man may sell his minor daughter as a maidservant. But the ancient oral interpretation, as expressed in the Talmud, expands on the purpose and parameters of this practice: a father may sell his daughter only when the family has reached a state of poverty so dire that the father has already sold his land, house, and even his last shirt. The ultimate purpose of the transaction is that the buyer or one of the buyer's sons will marry the girl; if they decide not to marry her, then the father must redeem her when he has the means. If she is neither married nor redeemed, she is free to go after six years of service or upon reaching her majority at age twelve — whichever comes first.

If the girl decides that she does not want to marry the master or his son, she has the right to refuse, and then she simply works out the remainder of the time on her contract. If she marries the master or his son, she must be treated with the full privileges of a wife. If the husband takes a second wife, he cannot diminish her status or his material support of her in any way. Again, this procedure is not recommended for most families, but only for situations of desperate poverty, where the father cannot provide for his daughter and seeks a better situation for her. Beyond that, marriages of minor children were not encouraged; nor should a young woman be forced to marry a man who does not please her. That culture recognized that a marriage is not likely to be successful unless both parties enter it freely.

ALTHOUGH THE PRACTICE of fathers selling daughters in marriage is unpalatable to modern sensibilities, it is important to note that even here the rules reflect the biblical respect for all people, even a person designated as a child maidservant. The law acknowledges her need to be protected, and by her marriage to be an important member of society. Perfection in life is sadly lacking. Yet people must do the best they can to live in a dignified moral way in an imperfect world. To the family in the direst poverty, the Bible offers a means to let a young daughter grow up in relatively beneficent circumstances and not be sent to the poorhouse or onto the street like Oliver Twist.

Ruth and Naomi (Ruth 1–4)

The theme of the book of Ruth is kindness and how it works itself out through a series of characters: Ruth, Naomi, Boaz, and the women of Bethlehem. It is kindness both between individuals (including the problematic relationship of daughter-in-law and mother-in-law) and at the level of community. An ancient maxim says that the Pentateuch begins as God's kindness to Adam and Eve and ends with God's kindness in burying Moses. It is no contradiction or diminishing of the kindness of Ruth and Naomi that their good acts eventually lead them from potential dissolution to a remarkable renewal in their lives.

Relationships between mother-in-law and daughter-in-law are notorious for backbiting and jealousy. Yet the biblical book of Ruth gives in four short chapters the narrative of in-laws who acted toward each other with the greatest kindness and respect. In this story, Naomi has moved with her prosperous husband and two sons from Bethlehem in Judah to Moab because there is a famine in Judah. Once they are there, unfortunately, Elimelech, Naomi's husband, dies. Once her sons come of age, they marry a couple of young women of Moab — Orpah and Ruth. But after only about a decade of married life, Naomi's two sons, Mahlon and Chilion, also die.

Now bereft of both family and wealth, and having heard that the famine is over in Judah, Naomi has determined to return to Bethlehem. Orpah and Ruth insist on accompanying her back to Judah. As much as Naomi can benefit from the support and companionship of the two young women, she nevertheless unselfishly urges them to return to their families of origin in Moab. Life would be very hard for poor women in an alien land; on the other hand, Orpah and Ruth will still have families in Moab and will find it easier to remarry. Orpah loves Naomi, but she can see the good sense of what Naomi is saying. She kisses Naomi goodbye and returns to her people.

Ruth, however, stays with Naomi, even though the latter still tries to dissuade her: "Your sister-in-law has returned to her people and her god. Follow your sister-in-law" (Ruth 1:15). Ruth replies to this with one of the most remarkable statements in the Bible and in the history of familial relationships: "Entreat me not to leave you, or to turn from you, for wherever you go, I will go, and wherever you lodge, I will lodge. Your people are my people and your God is my God. Where you die, I will die and there I will be buried" (1:16-17).

This beautiful expression of devotion reciprocates Naomi's magnanimity. Both Ruth and Naomi love and need each other, especially after having suffered such terrible losses; but even now, when she especially needs support, Naomi does not try to bind her daughters-in-law to herself, instead urging them to return to their own people and to the opportunity to remarry. Ruth loves and trusts Naomi and has come to admire her biblical qualities of character. And her speech here expresses her desire not only to move from Moab to Bethlehem but also to move from a Moabite way of life to a biblical one. For Ruth, the essence of biblical life is kindness, and she speaks of this life in terms of her love and devotion to Naomi.

As Naomi and Ruth finally approach Bethlehem, the women of the town come to look at them in disbelief. Can this be Naomi, who left Bethlehem as a prosperous and successful woman? Naomi answers: "Do not call me Naomi [sweet]. Call me Marah [bitter], for the Almighty has dealt very bitterly with me. Full I departed, and empty has God brought me back." This is not so much a complaint as perhaps an honest expression by a woman who has suffered much (1:20-21).

Ruth supports herself and Naomi by gleaning, picking up the small portions of grain that biblical law required harvesters to leave for the indigent. Her good character and her kindness to Naomi become known in Bethlehem, and those reports — along with the sight of a respectable and beautiful woman gleaning in his field — attract the attention of Boaz, who is not only a wealthy and dignified community leader but also a kinsman of Naomi's husband. When Naomi realizes that Ruth has made a contact with this relative of her husband, she plans to make a match between Ruth and Boaz — in order to give Ruth "a resting place which will be good for you" (3:1). For her part, Ruth remains devoted to her mother-in-law, who has acted so unselfishly toward her. But Naomi instructs Ruth on how to press her advantage with this prosperous man. Under her mother-in-law's instruction, Ruth stealthily lies down at the foot of Boaz's resting place, and when he awakes in the night and asks who she is, she says: "I am Ruth, your maidservant. Take your maidservant under your wing, for you are a close relative" (3:9).

Besides wishing to remarry for her own needs, Ruth also accepts the idea of marriage to a relative of her first husband (a so-called levirate marriage), so that the first son by Boaz will be regarded as a sort of replacement or continuation of her first husband. Boaz is a deeply empathic man who respects Ruth's refined character and is not put off by her foreign background. He also supports her wish to complete her kindness to her first husband. "And also Ruth the Moabitess, the wife of Mahlon, I have taken as wife to establish the name of the deceased on his heritage and that the name of the deceased will not be cut off from his brethren and from the gate of his place" (4:10).

After settling the potential claim (also under levirate law) of a closer relative to Elimelech before the elders of Bethlehem, Boaz marries Ruth, and in due course they have a son. The women of Bethlehem, acting almost like the chorus in a Greek drama, help to define for Naomi how this event has also brought her a large measure of restoration: "And the women said to Naomi, 'Blessed is the Lord who has not held back from you a redeemer today, and may his name be famous in Israel. And he shall be to you a restorer of the soul and to sustain your old age, because your daughter-in-law who loves you has borne him, and she is better to you than seven sons'" (4:14-15).

This child brings renewal to Naomi's life, almost as though he were a reincarnation of her sons. She feels rejuvenated, and she receives what is in essence the recognition of the people of Bethlehem. Naomi takes the infant into her arms, and the neighbor women again affirm her joy: "A son is born to Naomi." Scripture calls the infant by the name the neighbors give him — Obed, meaning "servant of God" (4:16-17). And though he is born to an alien woman, he becomes the father of Jesse, who is the father of King David.

Race and ethnicity are not important in the Hebrew Bible. Ruth is a Moabitess by birth and thus an alien in Judah, and at first it is not easy to adjust and find acceptance in a new society. Yet Boaz and Naomi, and finally the women of Bethlehem, recognize her fine character, and Ruth becomes not only a full-fledged Israelitess but an ancestress in the Davidic line of kings.

NAOMI'S WILLINGNESS to let Ruth live her life presents an obvious contrast to Laius, who is warned by an oracle not to let his son

Oedipus live because the latter might kill him; and it is a contrast to Clytemnestra, who attacks both her daughters, Electra and Iphigenia, for being disloyal to her, and binds them to herself (see the Epilogue). A failure to let a child develop can create a great deal of bitterness and resentment. An example of a mother's blocking her daughter from leading her own life is told in the 1993 Mexican film *Like Water for Chocolate*. Based on the best-selling novel by Laura Esquival, this fable from Mexico focuses on a young woman who discovers that her cooking has magical effects. The tale's heroine, Tita, is the youngest of three daughters in a traditional Mexican family. Bound by tradition to remain unmarried while caring for her aging, widowed mother, Tita nevertheless falls in love with the handsome Pedro. He returns her affection but cannot overcome her family's disapproval and instead marries Tita's elder sister. The lovestruck younger sister is brutally disappointed, and her sadness has such force that it infects her cooking: all of those who eat it feel her heartbreak with the same intensity.

The biblical mother-in-law Naomi does not act in this way. She understands Ruth's need to live her own life, and she pushes Ruth to remarry even if it means that she herself will be left alone. Ruth returns her kindness and respect by including Naomi in her life after she does remarry. No good can come from blocking a child's development. This does not mean that a mother should abandon a child, only that she should support the child's growth, and she will be amply rewarded.

CHAPTER 8

Women as Wives

M odern sitcoms no less than ancient Greek myths capitalize on
what is portrayed as an almost natural animosity and rivalry
between husbands and wives who are always sticking it to each other
and putting each other down. In the Bible, the first marriage was ar-
ranged by God himself, and marriage is considered the normal and de-
sirable state of being. Wives and husbands can build together, blending
their separate skills and strengths to make up a sum that is greater
than its individual parts. This chapter describes four marriages. Rachel
and Leah, the sisters who are two of Jacob's four wives, have a healthy
relationship with Jacob, though it is not without the tensions that were
always a part of polygamous marriages. The very independent Eve
compares favorably with the Greek Galatea, whose husband sought
total control over her. Another kind of spouse, Job's wife, is not supportive of her husband in times of challenge. In this chapter we also
look at some biblical laws about a couple remarrying after a divorce
— regulations that can help advance marital stability.

The Beloved and the Unloved:
Rachel and Leah (Genesis 29–31)

Any study of marriage in the Hebrew Bible is complicated by the fact that Scripture permitted polygamy, or polygyny. (*Polygamy* means having multiple spouses; *polygyny* means having multiple wives; in Hebrew society only the latter was really practiced.) This does not mean that every man took many wives. However, every man was entitled to by law, and many biblical stories speak of polygamous families (e.g., Abraham, Jacob, Elkanah, King David, and certainly King Solomon, with his 700 wives and 300 concubines). Sometimes the arrangements were harmonious, but often enough there was rivalry and conflict among the wives. Indeed, the Hebrew word for co-wife is *tsara*, meaning "enemy" or "trouble." Deuteronomy 21:15 declares that, if a man has sons from two wives, one of whom he loves and one whom he does not love, he must always give the firstborn's double portion of the legacy to the true firstborn, even if that son is the child of the wife that he does not love as well. We may note that the better-loved wife may more often, and quite naturally, be a later wife; for if a man has remained totally in love with his first wife, why would he have wanted another?

Although he is a biblical paradigm for greed and deceit, Laban of Haran has produced two fine daughters, Leah and Rachel, both of whom marry Jacob. Genesis 29 tells the story of Leah, Laban's elder daughter, a woman of high character who has watched as Jacob has worked seven years for her father in order to marry Rachel, her younger sister. A serious and sensitive woman who enjoys people, Leah is deeply concerned about marrying the right kind of man. She is perturbed to hear people suggest that, since her sister Rachel will marry Jacob, perhaps she should marry Jacob's brother, Esau: she is perceptive enough to know that this wild hunter would not be a good match for her. Nor will it be suitable to marry an idolater from among the men of her own town. A good marriage is so important to Leah that she is ready to participate in Laban's secret plan to use Rachel as bait for Jacob and to substitute herself for Rachel behind the bridal veil on the wedding night. Thus it is that she, too, will marry Jacob, albeit by a deception. She hopes that, despite everything, it will work out for the best.

Only upon rising from the marriage bed in the morning light does Jacob realize that his bride is Leah, not Rachel. He complains vigorously to Laban, who agrees to have another wedding a week later so that Jacob can marry Rachel as well, but he says that Jacob will have to work for him another seven years to fulfill his end of the bargain. Is Jacob angry with Leah as well as Laban because of the deception and the extra time he will spend working to earn Rachel? Jacob is not a hater by nature, and he probably has the personality to understand why Leah is so eager to marry him, why Laban wanted to marry off his elder daughter first, and even why deception is sometimes necessary to accomplish a worthwhile goal. Even so, on a personal level, he cannot be happy with his father-in-law.

An industrious and hard-working man, Jacob chafes under his father-in-law's shady character; then, as Jacob begins to prosper, he begins to notice that Laban's attitude toward him grows less friendly. God now appears to Jacob in a dream and instructs him to return to Canaan, his homeland, and God will be with him. Jacob calls Rachel and Leah to the field, where he can talk with them privately. He describes to them how loyally he has worked for Laban and how dishonest Laban has been with him. Yet God has been with Jacob, and his affairs have prospered. Now God has told Jacob to return to Canaan.

Rachel and Leah readily agree; their allegiance to Jacob is wholehearted. Laban has always treated them as if they were strangers, they say. Instead of supplying them with dowries, he has used them to gain Jacob's labor and has made them wait seven years to marry him. Laban has even taken the daughters' own money for himself (Gen. 31:15). Now they agree that Jacob must do as God has told him. Jacob and his family flee Laban's household while Laban is away shearing sheep. And Rachel steals Laban's *terafim,* apparently an oracular device, so that Laban will not have an easy time tracking them down once he learns that they are gone.

Scripture goes on to tell the story of the marriage from Leah's perspective. It says that Leah was *senu'a* ("hated," or "unloved," Gen.

29:31): "When God saw that Leah was *senu'a*, he opened her womb, while Rachel was barren." The wording may indicate not that Jacob hated Leah, but that she felt herself unworthy and unloved both because of her longtime fear that she would end up in an unsuitable marriage and because of the deception of Jacob that she has carried out with her father. Therefore, God now makes her fertile so that she bears four sons to Jacob within a relatively short time. This seems to be a clear indication from God of the propriety of Leah's behavior, and it helps remove any doubts Jacob may have had about her character. Leah goes on to have three more children with Jacob, and it is Leah beside whom Jacob later asks his sons to bury him in the cave of Machpelah in Hebron.

Significant also is the fact that the descendants of Leah's sons Levi and Judah later become the priests and kings of Israel. And though Jacob has a special love for Joseph and Benjamin, the two sons of Rachel, he also includes Leah's sons as full and eminent members of the covenant.

THIS STORY POINTS to the deep complexity of a marriage. Whatever its beginning, a marriage takes on a life of its own. And the very act of childbearing can transform a woman in her husband's eyes into a carrier of his progeny. By making Leah fertile and leaving Rachel infertile, God creates a new reality in the family. As the mother of his children, Leah is giving Jacob the gift of a future, and this must surely color his attitude toward her. This story also exemplifies the rights of a wife to the protection of her legacy. A man's affection and desire toward his wife may waver over the course of a marriage; yet a woman's honor and security are not held hostage. A classical Greek hero such as Jason could wholly reject his wife, Medea, and their children when he married a young princess. Jacob prefers Rachel to Leah, but he does not reject Leah, nor would Deuteronomic law have allowed it. It is against this background and within this context that the biblical family, including the practice of polygyny, must be understood.

Rachel and Leah are clear thinkers. They know that Laban has used them for his own gain, and they see clearly that their future lies in joining with Jacob to fulfill God's mission. They are not overtly disrespectful to Laban, but they know that they owe more to God and to Jacob than they do to Laban. They make a clean break with their father and go on to better things. This contrasts noticeably with stories in world mythology about fathers who literally sacrificed daughters for their own ends. A woman can be enmeshed with her father for many reasons (e.g., Antigone; see pp. 27-28, 45 above). If she is, she will find it difficult to cleave to her husband. Whatever Laban's faults — and they were obvious — his daughters were not enmeshed with him or emotionally enslaved by him. Rebecca's plan of sending Jacob to her family to find a wife has turned out to be very forward-looking and productive.

Job's Wife

The powerful story of Job recounts how a man is struck by terrifying misfortunes and yet never compromises his integrity nor ceases to search for meaning in the events of his life. Early in the story Job is dealt the blow of losing all of his great wealth and then all of his children. Later he is afflicted with severe skin inflammations all over his body, and he takes potsherds to scrape these inflammations and boils as he sits in ashes. Job's friends seem unable to understand what he is going through, and they become impatient with him.

What can one say to a man at this moment? The interpretive translation of M. Eisenmann in his monumental work on Job puts it this way: "His wife said to him, 'Are you still maintaining your unquestioning integrity? Blaspheme God and die!'" (2:9). Perhaps it is her own suffering that makes her speak this way, but Job's wife seems to want to rub salt in his wounds. No man feels completely forsaken as long as his loving wife is by his side. But Job's wife cannot understand or accept her husband's need to maintain his integrity in the face of events that seem to make it meaningless. What could Job's integrity signify in the face of such utter calamity? What would Job gain now even if he were still righteous? Better for him, in his wife's mind, to blaspheme God and die.

Job responds that he must accept whatever God sends and that his wife's suggestion is foolish. Perhaps his wife is at her wits' end, for she too has suffered much. Yet she shows little interest in seeking truth, and she does not support Job in his struggle. Her suggestion to Job to give up is pointless and expresses her own frustrations and fears rather than any interest in Job or in God. One is left to wonder whether Job's wife has been supportive of him in the earlier years when his family, business, and good deeds were all thriving. As long as she and Job were riding high, giving emotional and spiritual support seems to be less necessary — and much easier to do. When the old pleasures and successes are gone and mutuality is needed, all Job's wife can think of is for Job to die — and to die outside God's blessing.

THE STORY OF JOB and his wife painfully illustrates the conditional nature of the love some women have for their husbands: for example, they can forget the marriage vow they made to love their husbands "in sickness and in health." Job's wife seems angry at him for his misfortunes. Perhaps this comes out of her love for him, but it makes matters worse; the last thing Job needs is to be told to give up. This is not to idealize misfortune. Obviously, good fortune is better than bad, but both can and do come in a lifetime. Some women seem to thrive with a healthy husband, but others can reach out to one who is sick. It is important for a wife to support her husband in good times and bad, to be always conscious of the important emotional foundation she provides for her husband and family. This is a great power that women have, and they must use it wisely.

A man never needs his wife more than during hard times, times when he can feel that his whole life is a failure. Close friends may stay away, not visiting because they are somehow fearful that his misfortune is contagious. But such behavior is not appropriate for a biblical wife, because she shares a covenantal relationship with her husband. She should never detach herself from him and judge him as though he were an outsider. She must remain a full participant in their shared life.

Eve and Galatea

Two thousand years ago, the Roman poet Ovid recounted the myth of Pygmalion and Galatea. This story has been resurrected twice in the twentieth century: once as George Bernard Shaw's play *Pygmalion* and once as *My Fair Lady,* the hit Broadway musical of the 1950s. The mythical Pygmalion was so disgusted with women that he refused to marry, choosing instead to live alone. Meanwhile, he fashioned a marvelous ivory statue of a woman so beautiful that he fell in love with it himself. He caressed and kissed the sculpture, paying it compliments and bringing it gifts as though it were a real person. So Aphrodite, the goddess of love, granted Pygmalion's wish and brought the statue to life as Galatea.

Yet, as is so often the case, this superficially pleasant Greek myth has a cruel side to it. Some years later, Myrrha, a granddaughter of Pygmalion and Galatea, his former statue wife, falls passionately in love with her own father, Cyneras. She has an affair with him, always coming to him in the dark and never revealing who she actually is. One night Cyneras lights a lamp and, horrified by what they have done, draws a sword to kill her. She flees and turns into a tree. Cyneras, now anguished by his own guilt, kills himself (see p. 98).

Pygmalion is unable to relate to a woman unless he can not only totally control her but actually *create* her. She must have no identity beyond what Pygmalion gives her. He cannot trust her with any sort of freedom or self-motivation; he needs her to be beholden to him for everything — even life itself. Certainly, this lack of trust and the confusion of identity has led to the incestuous disaster story of Myrrha and Cyneras.

How different is the union of Adam and Eve at the beginning of the Bible's human narrative. Adam longs for a true companion in the newly created world; but rather than Adam's making a beautiful puppet that he hopes will be subservient to him, God is the one who creates the woman — not to be a puppet but a helpmeet-opposite. That is, she can be effective only by interacting with Adam as one strong person with another. Sometimes she must be straightforwardly helpful and supportive; but when the need arises, she must show her support by disagreeing with him — by being his "opposite."

There have always been and always will be men who select as mates women who seem beneath them in wealth, social standing, knowledge, or world experience. If a man does this hoping to control his wife, as Pygmalion hoped to control Galatea, he usually soon finds the "little woman" to be far less submissive than he expected.

WE CAN ONLY SPECULATE as to what Galatea's life with Pygmalion was like. He wanted her to be a puppet reflecting only his own needs and desires. This lack of individuation in Galatea may have been transmitted to their granddaughter, Myrrha, who, feeling inadequate to join with a husband, instead merges in sexual union with her father. When she turns into a tree in her attempt to escape, she goes back to the inert form from which Pygmalion fashioned Galatea. Cyneras may have been no different than Pygmalion: when he sees Myrrha pass out of his control by becoming a tree, he kills himself. Pygmalion's fascination with a sculpture reflects his underlying fear of change. Women, with their expressive and protean emotions, represent change to him and thus fear — and as such have to be subordinated. Galatea is Pygmalion's idealization of a woman rather than a real one. Western men have often fallen into this trap — of first idealizing and then subordinating women — so that women often feel that their men don't really know them.

This differs dramatically from the story of Adam and Eve, which expresses the biblical concept of a man "knowing" a woman both emotionally and sexually. Eve is no Galatea: she is an independent woman who eats of a tree but does not need to turn into a tree to escape Adam or God. She goes on to produce the human race, and Adam loves her as the mother of all things living and as a real human capable of change and growth.

Remarrying One's Wife (Deuteronomy 24)

Scripture ordains what seems to be a strange prohibition: a man may divorce his wife and remarry her, unless she has been widowed or divorced from another husband in between (Deut. 24:1-4). What might be the purpose of this law? Don Yitzhak Abarbanel was a great scholar of both the Bible and Greek literature, as well as a leading minister of the kings of Portugal and Spain. In his commentary on the Bible, he contrasts this law to a popular Greek idea of the community of wives that forms part of the basis of Plato's utopian republic. For his utopia, Plato planned that there would be no long-lasting nuclear families of steady father, mother, and children. Rather, the state would control the mating of adults according to its own interests, and the connection of a man and woman would not be permanent. The state would also control the raising of children, assigning them their places in society and their life's work as the state deemed useful. Plato greatly admired the constitution of the city of Sparta, in which men lived with other men in military barracks and visited their wives only by stealth. A Spartan man could also borrow his friend's wife, a form of wife-swapping.

Greek families were notoriously unstable; for example, unwanted infants were regularly left exposed to die. In Sparta the practice of infanticide was even worse: all infants had to be inspected by government officials, and those infants judged unfit for the rigors of Spartan life were dropped to their deaths from Mount Taygetus. Both families and individuals in Greece could suffer from a weak sense of identity and from a lack of belonging to something or someone. This would be especially true of the children emerging from such an unstable context. Anyone who works with young people in our society today knows how many of them feel a lack of security that comes from families that are broken or disrupted. As Abarbanel puts it, "such a child would be a stranger to everyone and not close to himself. He would never be sure who his father, mother or sibling would be." Indeed, this is one reason for marriages to be solemnized and celebrated in public and not in private — with only bride and groom present.

To Abarbanel, the biblical rule against remarrying one's wife if she has married someone else in between prevents legalized wife-swapping and helps to strengthen the family and develop the sense of identity, stability, and security for the husband, wife, and children. The next verse adds another law that would also have the effect of strengthening families: a man who has just married is not subject to military duty, or even to function as a supplier of provisions to the troops. Instead, he shall stay home and "bring happiness to his wife" (Deut. 24:5). Marriage is very important in biblical thought; in fact, it is so important that a new husband must put aside even national duties in order to devote himself to making his wife happy and to helping the marriage get off to a good start.

THE LAW ALLOWING SOMEONE to remarry his former wife — unless she has remarried someone else and is now divorced or widowed — is effective in two ways. First, it allows for the possibility of a resolution of misunderstandings that have led to the breakdown of a marriage in the first place. A husband and wife may feel that they have reached a dead end in their marriage; and the Bible does allow for divorce. Yet they may resolve that impasse, and the law allows them to remarry. At the same time, it does not see marital partners as interchangeable. This is reflected in the point that prohibits remarrying a former spouse who has since married someone else, pointing to the uniqueness of each individual in a marriage arrangement.

CHAPTER 9

Women as Mothers

"Do not forsake the teaching of your mother" (Prov. 1:8). The mother is a deeply respected and powerful figure in the biblical family model. It is very much her responsibility to help keep the children on the path of God's plan for history and to raise them to be wise and good. A task that is so difficult and so important requires a variety of skills and a strong measure of good character. This chapter includes the story of Rebecca, who understands the true needs of her two sons and her husband and uses her gifts as a diplomat to noble purpose. Jochebed's immense devotion helps to produce Miriam, Aaron, and Moses. Hannah's deep longing for a child is fulfilled, but she knows that the boy Samuel will need to move away from her, and she handles that need with devotion and grace. Sarah joins with Abraham to help establish a new monotheistic faith, and after giving birth to Isaac, she intervenes to protect their son and his own essential place in God's plan.

Rebecca (Genesis 25)

Rebecca was a great deal younger than Isaac, who was forty when they married, but it was a happy union in which both were supportive of each other and, it seems, even flirtatious (Gen. 24:63-67). But the first twenty years of their marriage were childless. Isaac already had received God's assurance that he would have children; but now it was unclear whether this would be with Rebecca or with another woman. In this story in Genesis 25, Isaac prays for his wife and she becomes pregnant. Her new condition brings her unusual pain; the two fetuses seem to be struggling inside her. Wondering what might be wrong, she consults a prophet, who tells her that she is carrying twins who will grow up to be very different kinds of people. Both of her children will found great nations, and they will be rivals of each other, just as the two inside her already seem to be vying with each other.

The story compares in a strange way to the Greek myth of the birth of Narcissus. A nymph, Liriope, is raped by the river god Cephisus, and she gives birth to a son. She goes to the prophet Teiresias and asks him how long the child will live. (Child exposure was practiced very widely in ancient Greece and not at all frowned on.) Liriope's question seems to imply the hope that a baby born in such unpleasant circumstances will not live. Teiresias's prediction is deliberately ambiguous, as his predictions always were, for he never truly meant to be helpful. "He [the boy] will be all right as long as he never knows himself." Ultimately, the boy, Narcissus, lives a short and unhappy life.

Rebecca's consultation with a prophet is more factual and helpful. She does, in fact, give birth to twin sons, Esau and Jacob. As they grow up, the differences between them begin to show: Scripture describes Esau as "knowing the hunt" and Jacob as "a simple man dwelling in tents" (i.e., a scholar, dwelling in the tent of learning). Isaac and Rebecca love both boys, but their relationships with their sons differ according to their individual personalities. Isaac has been losing his sight, and as he becomes more dependent, Esau brings him the fresh meat from his hunt. Esau has developed into the kind of man who lives his life by the cunning and force of the hunter. Isaac not only enjoys the meat, but is also perhaps drawn to Esau's athleticism. Furthermore, he may sense that, despite Esau's heroics as a hunter, he has great personal needs. Rebecca loves Jacob because she can see that it is he who will carry on the mission of Abraham and Isaac: he is a man of intellect and higher purpose, yet one who loves "simplicity" (Gen. 25:27) and not the skills of the chase or the battlefield. Perceptive as ever, Rebecca knows Esau's weaknesses and limitations, and she loves him nonetheless; but she understands Jacob's "simplicity" and goodness and prizes these virtues in him.

The years pass and Isaac, having lost his sight, decides to give the traditional father's blessings to his sons before his death (in fact, he lived many years after giving the blessings). Isaac will give to Esau the main blessing of both material well-being and spiritual mission (this blessing is distinct from the birthright); so he tells Esau to bring him some fresh venison as a preliminary meal for him before the blessing. Rebecca hears Isaac giving those instructions to Esau, and she knows well that the blessing should go to Jacob. Isaac may know that Esau has sold his birthright to Jacob, and thus he thinks that perhaps Esau needs the father's blessing more than Jacob does; or perhaps he simply intends his blessing for his firstborn son. Rebecca, however, sees more clearly: surely, she thinks, Jacob is the more spiritual son and hence should be given the main blessing and be entrusted with the continuance of Abraham's mission. Quietly but firmly, Rebecca convinces Jacob to join her in a plan by which he, instead of his brother, will receive Isaac's blessing. If they fail, Rebecca assures him, she will take all the responsibility. But the plan succeeds, and Jacob receives the main blessing. Esau receives a blessing more suited to the kind of man he actually is.

Rebecca manages to bring this about without demeaning Isaac and without causing a murderous conflict between her sons, both of whom she still loves and both of whom she is deeply concerned about. Hearing about Esau's murderous intent toward Jacob after he has lost the main blessing, Rebecca whisks Jacob off to stay with her brother Laban for a while, saying to him: "Why should I be bereaved of both of you in one day?" (Gen. 27:45). Rebecca handles this difficult situation with strength of character, calm wisdom, and a wholly positive attitude. She manages to provide both her sons with what they need and to treat her husband with great respect.

This is in stark contrast to the Greek story of Oedipus, the mythological king of Thebes. Oedipus is a basically decent man who has been fixed with a terrible fate — to murder his father and marry his mother. Learning that he has unwittingly done both, Oedipus blinds himself and later places a terrible curse on his two sons (who are also, of course, his brothers): that they should kill each other. This tragic curse is fulfilled. Rebecca manages to maneuver a very difficult situation so that her two sons receive individualized and suitable parental blessings. Her family is not destined to be cursed and destroyed, as Oedipus's family is, and her marriage remains harmonious.

REBECCA PERSONIFIES the biblical wife's vigorous application of wisdom. Though much younger than Isaac when they marry, she does not become merely an extension of her husband, but a great personality in her own right. Jocasta, Oedipus's mother/wife, is unable to prevent her tragic marriage to her son and what unfolds from that. Rebecca takes matters into her own hands and uses the skills of a brilliant family therapist. Jacob is not her favorite simply because she is more drawn to him; she knows that he is the right son to carry on the covenant. She also knows that Esau is the firstborn and her husband's favorite. So she seeks to take care of her family's future in a way that does not disrupt the present.

Although Rebecca devises a plan for Jacob to receive the main blessing, she realizes that Esau will be angry with Jacob, so she needs to enable Jacob to leave home and seek safety. She dovetails this with Isaac's desire to find Jacob a wife from among their family who live in Haran. Isaac wants Jacob to find a wife among their own people, and Rebecca wants him to live. So she sends Jacob to sojourn with her brother's family in Haran; as it turns out, she will never see him again. Rebecca's protective act is far different from the actions of many of the women of Greek literature, who see their children merely as extensions of themselves and their husbands merely as beings to manipulate for their own needs.

Jochebed (Exodus 2)

In 1940, a petite woman in her mid-thirties fled Europe with her husband and two small children in fear of the invading Nazis. Their long journey came to an end in Java, Indonesia, where the husband found employment as a teacher. But that peaceful interlude was all too brief. The Japanese attacked Pearl Harbor and then quickly overran Southeast Asia. The husband joined the Dutch forces and was captured by the Japanese. The woman and her two children were held in a different prison camp where, a month after they were incarcerated (March 1942), she gave birth to another little girl. People in the camps died quickly of starvation, torture, exposure, dysentery, beriberi, malaria, and typhoid. The woman did not know what had happened to her husband, and she had nothing to support her for the next three years but her own courage and her faith. She struggled and starved (her weight went down to 55 pounds) to keep her small family going. But she and her children survived and were liberated, and later they were reunited with their husband and father, who had spent most of that time in the infamous POW camp on the River Kwai. This kind of story is not unfamiliar during times of war and persecution; and this particular story is dramatically familiar and real to one of the coauthors of this book, Matthew Schwartz, because it is the story of his wife's family.

Let's go back 3,000 years. The Israelites suffered under the cruel bondage of Egypt, and then things got worse. The pharaoh decreed that newborn male babies should be thrown into the Nile River. Like the couple in 1940s Indonesia, Amram and Jochebed, a man and woman of the tribe of Levi, had a small son and daughter, but it seemed useless to have more children simply to see them destroyed. The couple may have even separated for a while; yet their faith was strong. In time, a third child was born to them, a son, who survived the dangers because he was aided by the love of his parents, a good-hearted Egyptian princess, and the working out of the divine plan. The baby who survived was Moses, the person God had chosen to lead the Israelites out of bondage and the leader who was to bring them God's commandments. In each of these stories, it is the faith and courage of one woman that enable the survival of many.

THE FIRST THEME of this story is Jochebed's courage and willingness to bear children given the dire threat to them. She is not operating out of a denial of reality but out of a deeper faith rooted in Scripture, the faith that one should pray and hope, even when the sword is at one's throat. God creates the plan of history, and no matter how bleak things seem, one must not lose hope.

The second theme is equally important. Like Rebecca and Hannah, Jochebed does not try to bind the young Moses to her. Though she undoubtedly loves him deeply, she lets him go and thus helps facilitate his adoption by the Egyptian princess Bithia. Note how different this is from the story of the adoption of Oedipus in opposition to the attempt to kill him by his mother, Jocasta.

A third theme is crucial: Jochebed becomes the nursemaid to her son, thus subordinating herself to his adoptive mother. Such an act is very difficult. It is in tune with the model of the true mother in the story of Solomon and the two women: the woman who is willing to give up her motherhood to save her son. This is the biblical model of woman as opposed to the Greek type of mothers — or indeed fathers — who will sacrifice a child for their own convenience.

Hannah (I Samuel 1–2)

Hannah was a very intelligent and able woman with a deep feeling of purpose: she wished to do something good with her life. But she was childless and she felt her lack deeply. She would journey annually with her husband, Elkanah, and her co-wife, Peninnah, and the latter's children to the sanctuary at Shiloh for the pilgrimage festivals. Elkanah loved Hannah very deeply and treated her with great affection and respect, but Hannah still felt sad when she saw Peninnah with her children. On top of that, Peninnah would mock Hannah severely about her childlessness, making her even more miserable.

After one of the festival meals in this story from I Samuel 1, Hannah goes alone to the sanctuary, and there she prays fervently to God for a child, promising that she will devote him to the service of God. Eli, the high priest, watches her as she prays, and he notices that her lips are moving but no sound is coming from her mouth. And she goes on like that for a long time. Thinking that she is drunk, Eli comes to reproach her. Hannah has great respect for the aged priest; but she is also intelligent, and she speaks to him straightforwardly. She explains her need to pray and even gently but firmly chides him for not perceiving that she is praying as a person in pain and not as one who is besotted.

Hannah has become miserable, but she prays for a child not merely out of vanity or personal need. Nor does she ask for a child of extraordinary beauty or brilliance — or even one who will carry on the family name. She wants a male child so she can raise him to serve God for his whole life, and in so doing she will fulfill her own purpose. In I Samuel 1:11, Hannah refers to herself three times as God's maidservant: "You will look at the affliction of your maidservant, you will remember me and not forget your maidservant . . . you will give your maidservant a man-child." Hannah's need for a child is expressed entirely in terms of her devotion to God and God's purpose.

By this time, Eli understands what manner of woman is standing before him, and he tells her that God will answer her prayer, though it is not clear whether he means this as a prophecy or simply a blessing. Hannah accepts Eli's encouragement and returns to the Shiloh festival in good cheer, hopeful for the fulfillment of her dreams. Indeed, before long Hannah becomes pregnant and gives birth to a son, and she calls this child Samuel, meaning "I have asked him of the Lord" (I Sam. 1:20). When the child is weaned, she brings him to Eli at Shiloh and reminds him of her vow to dedicate this child to God. She will leave the small boy Samuel to serve in the sanctuary, for, she says, "he is lent back to God." Samuel will be a child "special to God," she tells Eli, thus indicating that Eli should never punish him. God will take care of Samuel.

Scripture records Hannah's poem of praise and thanks to God (I Sam. 2:1-10):

> My heart has rejoiced in the LORD
> My horn is raised up by the LORD.

Hannah's main relationship is with God, and it is through him that she has found so much joy:

> None is holy like the LORD,
> For there is none besides you,
> And there is no rock like our God.

> For God is LORD of thought,
> And for him are deeds counted.

God knows all things and is concerned for everything in this world, which he rules. He is aware of all the things that people do: things that are lofty can be brought down, while those that are lowly can be raised up. Hannah was childless, and now she has a son.

> The pillars of the earth are God's,
> And he placed the world on them.

> The LORD will judge the ends of the earth.

Hannah ends with a prophecy of Israelite kingship:

> He will give strength to his king,
> And he will raise the horn of his anointed.

Beyond her own personal desire for children, Hannah's prophetic vision foresees a major shift in the life of the Israelite people. For some generations they have been led on and off by judges, but it is clear that now only a king will have the spiritual and temporal authority and dignity to rule in the way that is needed. Hannah realizes this and perhaps also foresees that her son will be the last of the judges and will anoint the first two kings of Israel: Saul and then David. Samuel is the important bridge between the old order and the new.

HANNAH FEELS STRONGLY that her child comes from God. Compare this to Eve's statement about Cain: "I have acquired a man from God" (Gen. 4:1). Eve says nothing when Abel is born. Only with the birth of her third son, Seth, does Eve fully acknowledge God's role in the birth of her child: "For God has given me another seed instead of Abel, for Cain slew him" (4:25).

Perhaps Hannah's long barrenness has made her more aware that her child is actually borrowed from God. This is crucial to the way children are raised. Eve's expression at Cain's birth seems self-centered, and Cain grows up with a sense of entitlement. He expects God to accept his offering and becomes infuriated that he does not get his own way. Cain is little interested in God, as though he is asking who God thinks he is not to accept his offering. Infuriated, he kills Abel, who does not approach God with this sense of entitlement.

A mother's attitude that a child belongs to her, or is an extension of herself, can lead to situations where the mother feels she has the right to control or even destroy her children, as Medea does in the Greek myth. When Eve gives birth to Seth, her third son, she acknowledges that God has given her this child, which is also Hannah's attitude: Samuel is lent to her by God, and she will return him to God with love.

Sarah (Genesis 16–18)

Sarah was Abraham's wife and coworker as together they introduced to the world radical new beliefs based on monotheism and on generosity and kindness toward fellow human beings. Sarah is sixty-five years of age when, following God's instructions, she and Abraham leave their home in Haran to journey to Canaan, "the land that I will show you" (Gen. 12:1). The years bring many challenges and dangers as the aging couple pursues their mission in an often inhospitable world. The couple remains childless for many decades, but finally, at the age of ninety, Sarah gives birth to a son, Isaac. The continuation of their work seems assured.

Sarah's place as a paradigm for biblical women is indicated in God's promise to Abraham (Gen. 17:15-16) that he should no longer call her Sarai ("my princess") but Sarah (i.e., Princess — in an ultimate sense). Proverbs 12:4 declares that an "excellent wife is the crown of her husband"; but in the Bible's larger view, she is much more. She is a princess and benefactress to the world and is fit, in her own right, to be a progenitress of kings and nations. This is not an injunction to show dominance over her husband; rather, it is an explanation of how important her work is both in support of her husband and in her own direct relationship with God. "And I will bless her and also give you a son from her; then I will bless her, and she shall be a mother for nations; kings of peoples will come from her" (Gen. 17:16).

What kind of woman was Sarah, and why did God, according to the Genesis narrative, see her as fit to be Abraham's beloved partner in their great work? She is described as very beautiful, and the Bible recounts her role in getting Abraham to take Hagar, her maid, as his wife so that Abraham may have children. And later, she plays a role in protecting Isaac from Hagar's son, Ishmael (see pp. 140-41). Yet there are surprisingly few incidents in which Sarah seems to play a specific role. Perhaps a key to understanding the meaning of Sarah's life is given in the complex sentence that describes her at the time of her death: "And the life of Sarah was one hundred years and twenty years and seven years — these were the years of the life of Sarah" (Gen. 23:1). Several scholars have seen in this verse the idea that Sarah's life has a unity of meaning and purpose similar to what the poet Wordsworth expressed in his poem "My Heart Leaps Up When I Behold."

> The child is father of the man
> And I could wish my days to be
> Bound to each other by natural piety.

Even at the experienced old age of one hundred years, Sarah has retained the guiltlessness of a seven-year-old and the enthusiasm of a twenty-year-old. Her life is a unified whole dedicated to the service of God. Sarah has lived fully in every stage of her life, conscious that each moment of her life has meaning, everything she does is important, and its organic pattern is being recorded in God's book of history.

THE EMPHASIS on the entire life of Sarah is in striking contrast to the Greek world, which idealized youth, and to the Stoic philosophers, who emphasized the moment of death. Certain events in the lives of the other matriarchs stand out. For example, as we have seen, Rebecca shines in the story of Jacob and Esau. But in Sarah's case, it is her whole life that illustrates her character; it is less any single event and more the continuity of her faith in her Creator and her love for Abraham and Isaac. Perhaps the full strength of a helpmeet-opposite cannot be measured in a single event. Sarah's strength is that she is there for the long term, through thick and thin, through good times and bad, as a lifetime partner through the many difficult tests that she and Abraham endure. One is reminded of Golda's response to her husband Tevye's question in *Fiddler on the Roof*: "Do You Love Me?" She initially declines to answer directly, in turn asking him rhetorically whether she doesn't bear his children, cook his meals, and wash his clothes. Perhaps women generally feel that their actions over the long haul speak more volumes than transitory words, and perhaps the story of Sarah is paradigmatic for understanding this aspect of a helpmeet-opposite: she is there for life.

CHAPTER 10

Women of the Home

There are women in the Bible who seek neither glory nor power but, while living quietly, contribute significantly to the well-being of their homes and their people — and they find fulfillment in doing so. The Shunemite woman of II Kings is content to "live among her people," but she plays a remarkable role in that story. Jael, praised by Deborah as "blessed above all women in tents," quietly strikes a warrior's blow for her people.

The laws of the "beautiful captive" instruct us on how to integrate this woman into the biblical home. Obadiah's wife locks herself and her children in her home to enable a miracle to be performed there. Hagar follows a different course: she leaves Abraham's home and faith for the remote spirituality of the desert nomad.

The Shunemite Woman (II Kings 4:8-37)

Scripture never gives the name of this woman from the town of Shunem, yet she is called a "great woman" (II Kings 4:8). She lives quietly with her husband, who seems to be a well-to-do farmer. The prophet Elisha often passes through this town, and when he does, she invites him in for meals. After a time, she suggests to her husband that they provide a room for the prophet where he can stay whenever he comes to town. Elisha appreciates the woman's kindness and offers to do her a favor in return. Does she need someone to speak for her to the king or the general? he asks. "Amongst my people, I dwell," she answers (4:13), indicating that she seeks no special favors. But Gehazi, Elisha's disciple, mentions to him that the woman is childless. The prophet summons her back. She stands at the door of the room, declining to enter his room out of modesty, and the prophet tells her that at this time next year, "you will embrace a son." Maybe she is overwhelmed by emotion: "Do not deceive your maidservant" (4:16), she responds to the prophet, perhaps contemplating the fact that "her husband is old."

The Shunemite woman is a remarkable person — independent and insightful, with a strong spirituality. It appears that she relates deeply, though at a respectful distance, to the prophet. Her husband seems to play a minor role in these events; though she also treats him with respect, she seems to understand that these are important matters that she must handle herself. Nor is she arrogant: her remarks (4:13) indicate that she is happy to see herself as just another person among her people, and she does not seek more than that.

The child is born as the prophet has foretold. Several years later, on a day when the boy has gone out to the field with his father and the harvesters, he suddenly becomes ill, crying, "My head, my head." His father has him taken to the house, where he lies in his mother's lap for several hours and then dies. Somehow the mother knows what to do; though she is a woman of deep emotions, she stays cool in a crisis. First, she lays the child down on the prophet's bed, expressing in that act her faith in God. Then she goes to find Elisha, who is at Mount Carmel, and bows before him, grasping his feet as a supplicant would.

Gehazi steps toward her to move her away, but the prophet says, "Leave her alone, for her soul is in deep distress." Gehazi is a smart enough man, but he cannot tune in to the high level of understanding of the Shunemite woman, and she knows it. Earlier, when Gehazi had gone ahead of Elisha to welcome her, she told him nothing of why she had come; nor did she tell her husband where she had gone or why.

But she relates to Elisha — who immediately sees that she is soul-sick, though God has not revealed to him why. The Shunemite woman reminds Elisha about his original promise and prophecy: "Did I ask a son of my lord? Did I not say, 'Do not mislead me'?" The prophet sends Gehazi ahead to heal the boy with his (Elisha's) walking staff, telling him to focus on his mission and not to talk to anyone. But Gehazi seems to take the whole matter lightly, perhaps doubting that the prophet can actually revive the child or perhaps boasting to passersby about the great healing *he* was about to perform.

Gehazi comes to the prophet's bed in the Shunemites' home, where the boy is now lying, and places Elisha's staff on him, but the boy remains lifeless. Elisha follows soon afterward, and Gehazi reports that the boy has not been revived. Elisha sees for himself — perhaps realizing for the first time that the boy is actually dead — and closes the door so that the ongoing miracle will not become a public matter. He prays and then lies down on the boy, mouth to mouth, eye to eye, and palm to palm. Perhaps Elisha is trying some resuscitation technique, but underlying this intervention is his prayer to God. The boy's body soon begins to warm, and he sneezes seven times, indicating that the body's system is working again.

Elisha calls to the Shunemite woman to pick up her son. She bows to the ground to honor the prophet and lifts up her son. There is no record that she utters a word at that moment. It is not necessary; her silence expresses with great eloquence the depth of her faith.

THIS STORY REFLECTS the natural human tendency of a person who is promised something she has longed for to fear that, once it has been given, it can just as easily be taken away. The Shunemite woman's faith is strong enough to believe Elisha's prophecy; but she correctly intuits that the prophecy does not ensure her child's health. When the boy comes in from the hot sun complaining that his head aches and then he stops breathing — possibly from heat stroke — her deepest fears seem to be realized. Yet she neither lashes out at Elisha nor renounces her faith, but maintains her hope with quiet dignity. Elisha is moved by the entire situation and prays to bring the boy back. He had never meant for his promise to be empty, but sometimes life's real test comes after a person thinks she or he has arrived. Passing the second test can be the real mark of faith.

Hagar (Genesis 16)

The ancient Roman historian Livy wrote that Julius Caesar and his aides once passed through a small town and wondered whether this little place was home to the same sorts of political intrigue and conflict that Rome itself was. Caesar responded that he would rather be the number-one man in this little town than the number-two man in the whole empire.

Hagar is a woman who, like many biblical figures, faces a certain window of opportunity. Egyptian in origin, Hagar has become Sarah's maidservant in Abraham's household. Scripture does not describe her appearance, but perhaps she looked like the Egyptian women portrayed in the wall paintings and statues of that period. In this story from Genesis 16, Abraham and Sarah have been married for years but have no children. God has promised that their children would be as many as the stars of the heavens and the sands of the seashore, but Sarah isn't sure whether the promise to Abraham will be fulfilled through her or through another woman. When she seemingly despairs of bearing a child herself, she brings Hagar to Abraham and encourages him to marry her, hoping that "perhaps I will be built up through her." This practice was not unusual in the societies of the ancient Near East; it is similar to today's practice of childless couples adopting a child. Nonetheless, Abraham is very reluctant, for he loves Sarah deeply.

Did Sarah pick Hagar because of some special merit in her, or did she choose her as the simple bearer of a child whom Sarah would then raise as though it were her own? The ancient Midrash suggests that Hagar was an Egyptian aristocrat, a princess who joined Abraham's household when Abraham was in Egypt because she was impressed by his monotheistic beliefs. So Abraham does take Hagar as a second wife, and she soon becomes pregnant, at which point "her [Hagar's] mistress became light in her eyes." Sarah is not the saintly woman she appears to be, Hagar thinks; otherwise God would have answered her prayers for a child long ago. Now Hagar acts in a demeaning manner toward Sarah rather than treating the latter as a mentor and senior partner. Sarah complains to Abraham: she has acted nobly in encouraging him to take a second wife, so why is she now so "despised in [Hagar's] eyes"? Abraham says that Hagar is her maidservant, so Sarah may do what she wants to. Sarah becomes tougher with her maidservant, and Hagar flees into the desert.

What has happened to Hagar? Perhaps she sincerely believes that Sarah is not what she seems, or perhaps she can't resist showing off her new status as Abraham's wife — and a pregnant one to boot. But perhaps, too, as much as she likes the new position, she is beginning to chafe at some the more demanding responsibilities and obligations that her new status requires. While she is in the desert, a place of wild freedom, an angel meets her with a message from God. Whatever her faults, Hagar is a spiritual woman who is capable of having visions of angels. The angel tells her to return and submit to Sarah as her mistress. Hagar will bear a son, says the angel, who would be the father of a mighty nation. She is to name him Ishmael, "for God has heard your pain. And he will be a wild ass of a man, his hand against everyone and everyone's hand against him." Ishmael would indeed be a vigorous and aggressive man who loved the wildness of the desert.

Hagar, sensitive and emotional, has become very disturbed by Sarah's treatment of her, but now she takes strength from the fact that God is watching her and recognizing her feelings even in the desolation of the desert. She refers to God here as "the God who sees" (16:13), and she calls the nearby well "the well of the God who is seen here" (16:14). Hagar returns to Abraham's tents, where she soon gives birth to Ishmael. Fourteen years pass, and finally — miraculously — Sarah, at age 90, gives birth to Isaac, whose father, Abraham, is 100 years old. At about the time that Isaac is weaned, Sarah becomes concerned about Ishmael's wild and cynical behavior and the possibility that he will try to influence or hurt Isaac — even kill him. Ishmael does not wish to be simply Isaac's brother and ally; he seems driven to be in charge. Sarah can see that Ishmael is not the one who is ready to carry on Abraham's divinely appointed mission. And indeed, God has appointed Isaac, not Ishmael, to become the bearer of that mission and purpose.

"Drive out the maidservant and her son," she says to Abraham, who is very disturbed at the idea. But God himself speaks to Abraham, assuring him that Sarah is entirely correct, and that he must follow her demands. God also assures Abraham that Ishmael will do very well for himself. So Abraham gives provisions to Hagar and Ishmael and sends them away.

Again, Hagar seems to go into a spiritual crisis, perhaps regretting that she ever left the comfortable polytheism of her childhood. Perhaps, too, she resents her son for causing them to be driven out of Abraham's household. Instead of going to a settlement, she wanders in the desert until the water Abraham has provided gives out. Ishmael is ill, and Hagar, unable to deal with his problems in addition to her own confusion, places Ishmael under a bush and sits down some distance away. Weeping from sheer frustration, and unwilling to watch him weaken and die, she probably feels that this is an act of proper sensitivity on her part; but any good mother should have stayed to give the boy whatever help or comfort she could. Still, God hears Ishmael's cry and sends an angel to show Hagar a well nearby. Ishmael survives and grows up to become a strong man and a warrior. And Hagar, in a sense true to her origins, finds him a wife in Egypt, her own homeland.

HAGAR POSSESSED qualities of intelligence and spirituality, plus an independent spirit; but she could also become jealous and overbearing. She found it hard to tolerate and submit to authority, even when it was fully legitimate. Independence is a powerful quality, but at times it must be limited.

This story turns on two related issues: (1) the difference between seeing and hearing, and (2) the difference between Hagar's sensitivity and Sarah's. It is significant that, though Hagar names her son Ishmael ("God will hear") at the angel's behest, she is more inclined toward seeing as her mode of perception and comprehension. She names both her vision of God and the well where this takes place in terms of the seeing mode. But there is a fundamental difference between seeing and hearing: hearing involves a two-way communication. God hears humans, and humans hear God (even the giving of the Ten Commandments at Mount Sinai was described in an aural rather than a visual mode), and the angel tells Hagar to name her son accordingly. But Hagar, true to her Egyptian roots, is dominated by the visual mode of apprehension. She wants God to "see" her son as one can see God. "Seeing God," however, is foreign to the biblical world, where graven images are forbidden. She wants God to see her in the sense of being noticed, but she has less conception of God hearing her in the sense of being understood.

If God hears her, she must open herself to hear God, and this she cannot do. She has problems with authority all through the story. Sarah is very different: she hears the need for Abraham to have a successor, and she puts her own personal dreams and discomforts aside to facilitate Hagar's bearing a child to Abraham. This is strong devotion to the covenant. Yet when she sees Hagar being disrespectful, she reacts not merely out of personal pique but from a sense that Hagar may not fit into the Abrahamic mission and purpose. She gets a heightened sense of this when she herself miraculously becomes pregnant: she now knows that Isaac, not Ishmael, will be the heir to the covenant.

Sarah knows this not merely from a sense of maternal protectiveness but from her deeper *hearing* of God's mission. She remains willing to allow Ishmael to stay in the household until she realizes that Ishmael is a threat to Isaac and the divine plan. She then feels that she must urge Abraham to send Ishmael and Hagar away, not as an act of revenge but for the sake of their calling and God's covenant. Hagar's sensitivity is quite different: it is more the sensitivity of feeling personally slighted by Sarah and less a sensitivity to the larger purpose of Abraham's life and her place in it. She could have stayed with Abraham and Sarah and lived in harmony, but Hagar was so busy "seeing" and "being seen" that she could not "hear" or "be heard."

Deborah, Jael, and Sisera's Mother (Judges 4–5)

The book of Judges narrates a story involving three women: Deborah, Jael, and Sisera's mother. The first was a prophetess and a judge of Israel, the second was a simpler woman of fine character, and the third was utterly heartless. The second half of the narration (Judges 5) is in Deborah's own words, giving us a feeling of being very close to this unusual woman.

After settling in the promised land of Israel, the Israelites lived in a rather loose alliance of their twelve tribes. There was neither king nor political center, and in a series of incidents where the Israelites behaved wickedly, God allowed them to fall into the hands of powerful enemies — Ammonites, Midianites, and others. In Judges 4, the conqueror is King Jabin, a Canaanite whose army has nine hundred iron chariots at its disposal and is led by Sisera, a hard and brutal general. Jabin has cruelly oppressed the northern tribes of Israel for twenty years. It is a time of great danger for the Israelites: people have come to live in fortified cities and are afraid to travel. Yet there is one ray of hope: a remarkable woman, Deborah, serves her people as a prophetess and leader, dispensing wisdom and judgment from under a palm tree on Mount Ephraim.

In what is perhaps a play on words in this narrative in Judges 4–5, the Bible calls her the "wife of Lapidot," which could just as well mean "fiery woman." Deborah keeps the moral spirit and teachings alive among her people during this difficult time. She sees herself as "a mother in Israel," meaning that she is supporting and teaching her people, loving them as a mother would a child. Heeding a command from God, she calls Barak ben Abinoam and tells him to gather 10,000 men to go with him to Mount Tabor in the lower Galilee. There, near the brook Kishon, God will draw in Sisera with all his chariots and men and will deliver them into Barak's hands.

Barak hesitates. He says that, unless Deborah agrees to go with him, there is no purpose in his going. Deborah assures Barak that she will indeed accompany him, but she warns him that he will receive little personal glory because God is going to deliver Sisera into the hands of a woman. Sisera learns of Barak's movements and leads a strong force to Mount Tabor. Deborah now comes to Barak with the message that God has given the Canaanites into Barak's hand. "And the Lord confused and routed Sisera and all the chariots and all of the camp with the edge of the sword before Barak" (4:15). God sends the Canaanites into a panic, and there isn't much of a battle. "From heaven they fought, the stars from their courses fought against Sisera. The brook Kishon swept them away" (5:20-21). In her poetic song in Judges 5, Deborah depicts the forces of nature attacking Sisera. It is a curious fact that 2,900 years later, Napoleon Bonaparte won a battle against the Turks near Mount Tabor, a victory that was aided by the Kishon's flooding over the Turkish army in a storm.

Shaken by the sudden collapse of his powerful army and vaunted iron chariots, Sisera flees on foot, perhaps fearing that his chariot will be too recognizable. He ends up at the tent of Jael, the wife of Heber the Kenite, with whom Jabin and Sisera are on good terms. The Kenites were nomadic tent-dwellers, a branch of the family of Jethro, Moses' father-in-law. Jael comes out to meet Sisera and urges him to hide in her tent: "Turn, my lord, turn to me. Do not fear." Perhaps Sisera thinks that he can hide better in a woman's tent, or perhaps he feels the need for a woman in this time of intense danger. In any case, he enters Jael's tent, and she covers him with a large woolen garment.

Sisera asks Jael for water to quench his thirst, but she gives him milk instead, knowing that the drink and the warm garment will make him drowsy. She agrees to his demand that, if his pursuers come while he is resting, she will tell them that she has seen no man. But as Sisera sleeps, Jael stealthily takes a tent peg and a hammer; she cannot grab a knife or sword, for if Sisera were to awaken, he would guess her purpose. She takes the tent peg and hammers it into the temple of this powerful man, right through his head and into the ground below. When Barak comes in pursuit of Sisera, Jael simply shows him the body of Israel's enemy in her tent. Jael is not a warrior; she is a quiet woman who is content to live with her family. Yet she does not hesitate to strike a warrior's blow for her God and his people when push comes to shove. Her act is the crowning blow in Israel's complete victory over and destruction of the Canaanite army.

Deborah composes a great hymn (Judges 5) to commemorate this crucial moment in Israel's history and to express Israel's love for God more than for victory and spoils. She describes the decline of life under Jabin's rule and the unwillingness of some Israelites to break out of it. She recalls the great revelation of the law at Mount Sinai and how the earth itself trembled and the clouds and mountains reacted to the close presence of God. The Israelites, though oppressed, still did not give up hope. Many bravely joined Barak to fight against Sisera, notably the tribes of Zebulon and Naphtali; some of the tribes did not, preferring to remain in the apparent comfort and safety of home. Deborah praises Jael, whom she understands with a special empathy as a woman: "Blessed above women shall be Jael, wife of Heber the Kenite. By women in the tent shall she be blessed" (5:24).

Judges 5:28 introduces Sisera's mother, the third woman in this story. In contrast to the showing of wisdom and good character by Deborah and Jael, Sisera's mother peers through the window and moans as she awaits the return from battle of her warrior son. Worried because he is late getting home, she looks for the chariots that never will come. She calms her anxiety when she thinks that it must be taking the army a long time to gather and divide up all the spoils. Certainly, every man must be taking an Israelite woman for his bed, or perhaps a few women. Sisera's mother shows no respect or empathy toward what she imagines will be the women captives. She uses a vulgar and demeaning term to describe them *(raham rahamataim),* and her attitude is a manifestation of a cruel and evil way of life, which God deplores. Deborah says: "So may perish all your enemies, O LORD. And may those who love Him be as the sun when it goes forth in its strength" (5:31).

THIS STORY DRAMATIZES the differences between two basic types of women who are on the home front. The first type, represented here by Deborah and Jael, are peace-loving women who, when faced with a crisis, rise to the occasion, not from blood lust, inhumanity, or desire for power, but to defend their own people and to fulfill God's purpose. There is no indication that either Deborah or Jael is seeking power. Indeed, when Barak requires Deborah to come to the battle with him, she warns him that people will attribute his victory to a woman. Jael is described as a "woman in the tents." She has no interest in power or killing; but when Sisera falls into her hands, she does what needs to be done: she kills him quietly and with no pomp or celebration. The wise leadership of Deborah and the heroic act of Jael help bring peace to Israel for forty years.

Sisera's mother is a totally opposite figure. Her love for her son seems preoccupied with thoughts of glory — looting and spoils, conquest and power. This is what she wants for her son. As she shows in her demeaning and derogatory speech, Sisera's mother seems to have no empathy for other women — such as Deborah shows to Jael — and no real love for her son either, other than wanting conquest and power for him.

Yefat Toar (Deuteronomy 21)

In the 1970s a gripping movie was made from Euripides' play *The Trojan Women*, starring some of the world's leading actresses — Katharine Hepburn, Irene Pappas, and Vanessa Redgrave. It is the story of the women of Troy, now captives of the cruel Greek foes who have slaughtered their husbands and sons and laid waste to their city. Women who had been queens and princesses will now be slaves and concubines in the homes of their enemies. Indeed, the basic issue in the *Iliad* is the great dispute between Achilles and Agamemnon over which warrior should take which captive women as his trophies.

The book of Deuteronomy prescribes its own rules for the treatment of women captured in war (Deut. 21:10-14). Unfortunately, war brings about a state of emergency in which kings and generals cannot be held to the usual dignity, diplomacy, and legalities of peacetime. In the rage of battle, when human life is cheap and brave warriors feel the intensity of primitive urges, what are the women to do? Women have always followed armies to do the soldiers' laundry, to nurse the sick and wounded, and to serve as prostitutes. They would often dress in such a way as to attract the soldiers who won the battle. The Bible recognizes the realities of the battle situation in its rules on how to treat female captives, though commentators disagree on some of the details.

The biblical Israelite went to battle as a messenger of God. Yet he could also, of course, be caught up in the raging tide of blood and violence. The Western mind associates prowess, whether military or athletic, with sexual success. The pretty girls crowd around the hero who scores the winning touchdown, not around the players of the losing team. And it is certainly true in war: the winning hero attracts the women. Indeed, the aggressive energy of the victor has a strong sexual element. If one meets these captives or camp women and is overwhelmingly attracted to one of them, how should a soldier act? The law in Deuteronomy 21 offers a method that seeks to combine reality with humanity: the soldier may take one of these female captives *(yefat toar)*, but he must bring her to his home, where she must stay for a month to mourn the separation from her family and her old way of life. Then the man may marry her. Commentaries disagree about whether sex may take place once before this formal marriage, and also about whether she may or may not be taken against her will. A soldier may not take more than one such captive, nor may he take more women for his father, brothers, or friends. The captured woman is not simply a chattel or a toy.

The Deuteronomic law sets up the month-long period for the soldier to cool down and for the captive woman to adjust. If the man is already married, it is clear that his previous wife (or wives, because the culture was one of polygamy) will help him regain his composure. The *yefat toar* spends this period in a domestic setting, which serves as a training course in Israelite life. The man, though permitted in most interpretations to have intercourse with her one time before marriage, is still not given total license. He must go on to marry her and may not simply abandon her when he grows tired of her. If he does not desire to marry her, he must set her free; and he certainly is not allowed to sell her. The injunction ends by addressing the man not to "treat her brutally, because you have humbled her" (Deut. 21:14).

THE LAWS IN DEUTERONOMY hoped that all these rules and safe-guards, even possibly cohabiting with the woman once before marriage, would help the soldier regain his self-control and would help to prevent a relationship that could be very hurtful in the long run. The law emphasizes the dignity of the captive woman: though her captivity is a reality, she must still be treated with some respect. She is not a free woman and not the victor in the war, but she is a human being.

The biblical mindset avoids the false antithesis between perfection and annihilation. It might be tempting to give a captive woman no consideration whatever, to deny her status as a person, to essentially say that, if she is not fully free, she is not human at all. Biblical law recognizes that this captive has lost her freedom, but she has not lost her humanity, her dignity, or her status as being created in God's image. She has lost something, to be sure, but not everything.

Obadiah's Wife (II Kings 4)

So many times in the Bible, a seemingly small and isolated incident seems to lead to much greater things. "And a certain woman from among the wives of the disciples of the prophets cried out to Elisha saying, 'Your servant my husband is dead, and you know that your servant feared God; and now his creditor is coming to seize my two boys as slaves [to pay off our debts]'" (II Kings 4:1). The Bible does not give the woman's name, but very ancient tradition recorded both in the Midrash and in Josephus's *Antiquities* identifies her as the widow of Obadiah, an officer of King Ahab of Israel and a righteous man who had secretly supported a hundred disciples of the prophets when evil Queen Jezebel was persecuting adherents of the God of Israel.

Perhaps the woman would not have sought help for a more mundane problem, but now she fears that her sons can be taken away and placed in a godless and harsh environment so unlike everything to which her husband has devoted his entire life. It is precisely because Obadiah had borrowed money to sustain the scholar-prophets he supported that the little family is now in such dire straits. She reminds the prophet of this: "Your servant, my husband. . . ."

The prophet asks the woman what she has in the house. There is only one small cruse with a little oil in it. Yet even from so little can great things come. Elisha instructs her to borrow containers from her neighbors — as many as she can. Then she should close her door on herself and her sons and pour from her little cruse into all the others. The woman does so, and the small pot pours oil until all the containers are filled, at which moment the oil ceases to flow. The prophet then instructs her to sell the oil, pay her creditor off, and use the rest to support her family.

The story contrasts strangely with the events of the preceding chapter, in which a king of Moab has been besieged in his city by the united armies of Judah, Israel, and Edom. In utter despair, he sacrifices his son as a burnt offering to his god, thus essentially destroying his future and his present in one moment. There were problems in Israel, too, and the cruel persecutions by the dowager queen, Jezebel, had brought misery and danger to the followers of the true God. Yet people such as Obadiah's widow would stand steadfast, each in a small way, to do what was right, and God would help them. This narrative in II Kings 4 is the first of several stories about the prophet Elisha: taken together, they show a series of small events that involve seemingly small and insignificant people who help to maintain the biblical faith and mission.

THIS STORY EXEMPLIFIES the importance of small, concrete things. Women can at times be made to feel diminished for concentrating on the events of daily life — cooking, cleaning, preparing clothes for the children, pouring oil — at the expense of contemplating more abstract and "momentous" matters. The abstract has, indeed, been elevated by Western thinkers. Yet part of the genius of the Bible is its awareness that the material and the spiritual are not in opposition to each other, and the Bible respects women's awareness of this, though it has been criticized harshly for this view by Western thinkers. (Voltaire, for example, attempts to ridicule the Hebrew Bible for its law commanding the proper burial of one's excrement (Deut. 23:13-14). "Is it possible," Voltaire asks, "that God prescribed to the Jews how they should relieve themselves in the desert and concealed from them the dogma of a future life?"[1] One might ask how many lives were saved during the bubonic plague by sanitary laws such as those found in the Bible, and how many by the intellectual arrogance of people like Voltaire.) Western thought often prefers great and lofty ideas with empty actions, such as those of the Moabite king. It is part of the insight of women to emphasize the concrete details of life, and Obadiah's wife exemplifies this.

1. Voltaire, quoted in Lev Shestov, *Athens and Jerusalem,* trans. Bernard Martin (Athens, OH: Ohio University Press, 1966), pp. 128-29.

Rejecting One's Mission

"Labor not to be rich, cease from thine own wisdom" (Prov. 23:4). At some time in their lives, all people encounter a choice between accepting and rejecting their life's mission. Some very talented women whose stories are told in the Bible reject what might have been a very positive mission and instead follow ephemeral and destructive goals. Queen Jezebel is a prime example. Highly talented and yet manipulative, she arranges the false accusation and death of an innocent man in order to acquire yet another vineyard for an already rich throne. The necromancer of Endor is also a woman with considerable sensitivity and intuition, but she uses this talent in a forbidden occupation that violates biblical commandments. The wife of Potiphar is another attractive and capable woman; but she uses her charm in an effort to seduce Joseph, himself a man with a mission, even though it entails being unfaithful to her own husband. When Joseph rejects her, Potiphar's wife continues her destructive behavior and falsely accuses him to her husband. Finally, Lot's wife does not follow God's warning to leave the immoral Sodom; unable to separate from the city, she is turned into a pillar of salt.

Jezebel (I Kings 21; II Kings 9)

The ancient Phoenicians worshiped many nature gods, such as Baal and Astarte, often engaging in violent, orgiastic rites that included child sacrifice and temple prostitution. Even so, King Ahab of Israel took a Phoenician princess as his principal wife: Jezebel was not only the daughter of King Ethbaal of Sidon but also a fanatical idolatress. Jezebel established the Phoenician cults in her husband's realm, importing hundreds, perhaps thousands, of idolatrous priests to do her work; not content to stop there, she persecuted the followers of the one true God. Ahab still felt some attachment to the faith of Israel, but most often he willingly followed his wife (I Kings 21:25). Jezebel led her husband into forms of idol worship that the Israelites had never seen before, and Ahab, as usual, went along.

Jezebel came from a culture that had different views of kingship than the Israelite monarch did. The Phoenician king's main aim was to add power, glory, and wealth to himself; a biblical king, quite to the contrary, was supposed to lead his people in living according to God's teachings. The story of Naboth's vineyard seems to set a pattern and tone for Ahab's reign, during which Jezebel could plan and manipulate and deceive to gain whatever she wanted.

In this story in I Kings 21, Naboth is the owner of a fine vineyard adjacent to one of Ahab's palaces in Jezreel, and Ahab wishes to buy the vineyard. But Naboth refuses to sell, telling the king that he could never sell property that he has inherited from his fathers through many generations. Ahab returns home angry and sullen, going to his bed and refusing to eat. But Jezebel easily pries from her husband the reason for his sullenness: Naboth has refused to sell him the vineyard. Ahab does not mention the religious scruple, well established in Hebrew law, about selling inherited land, perhaps because he is ashamed to seem weak in front of his Phoenician queen. Jezebel tells Ahab that he has to be strong to be a king; she assures him that she will be able to take care of everything, in essence letting him know that she can be strong even when he is weak. And she does take care of everything — in her own ruthless manner. She arranges for two "scoundrels" to falsely come before the elders and accuse Naboth of blaspheming God and the king; consequently, Naboth is stoned to death. Jezebel then informs Ahab that Naboth is dead and that the vineyard, as the property of an executed criminal, reverts to the king.

As Ahab goes to the vineyard to take possession of it, God sends Elijah the prophet to confront Ahab. Ahab's declared enemy, Elijah, fearlessly tells the king that, because of this crime against Naboth, "in the place where dogs licked the blood of Naboth, so the dogs will lick your blood as well" (I Kings 21:19). Ahab still respects the word of a prophet, and he dons sackcloth and fasts to show his contrition. God informs the prophet that, because of Ahab's contrition, he will not take the kingdom away from him; God will bring that calamity during the reign of his son. In the meantime, however, Elijah's prophetic curse against Jezebel ("The dogs shall eat Jezebel by the wall of Jezreel" [21:23]) remains in effect.

Years later, relying on the prophecies of Elisha, Jehu, an army general, murders King Jehoram, Ahab's son and successor, and moves swiftly on to Jezebel's palace in Jezreel (II Kings 9). Even in facing the coup that would topple Ahab's family from rule, Jezebel remains astonishingly cool — every inch the queen. She dresses well, puts on her makeup, and stands defiantly at an upper-story window. Perhaps, with this show of queenly disdain, she hopes to retain the loyalty of her own people and to face down Jehu. As Jehu approaches the palace, she calls out to him, reminding him of the failed plot of Zimri against King Elah years before.

But Jezebel's bravado, though somewhat impressive, does not prevail. Jehu calls to the servants who are no longer faithful to her to throw her out of the window. After they do, her corpse lies on the ground while the horses of Jehu and his men trample it going in to take over the palace. Jehu has lunch before he thinks about Jezebel again; but after a time, he tells his men to go out and bury the "accursed woman." After all, she was the daughter of a king. But when Jehu's men go out to the wall, they find only her hands, feet, and skull; the rest of her has been eaten by dogs, as Elijah had prophesied years before (II Kings 9:35-37).

Did Jezebel have a good side to her as well? Strangely, a Midrash relates that Jezebel would step out of her palace to join in wedding or funeral processions that were passing by the palace. Perhaps an interest in marriage and death are common to all people — to fanatical idolaters as well as Israelite monotheists.

JEZEBEL WAS a woman of ability and power, and had she stayed in her native Phoenicia, she would likely have been a very successful queen. Yet her sense of purpose is very unlike the great women of the Bible. Rather, Jezebel is in the world of Delilah and Zeresh, the wife of Haman. She is attractive and ruthless and can manipulate her husband for her own ends. He may interpret this strength as loyalty to him, though it would cause his downfall. Jezebel is like Lady Macbeth, so driven by ambition that she can destroy everything she touches — including, ultimately, herself. The fact that she is not an Israelite and thus does not have the covenant, mission, and purpose of the biblical God bred in her bones is not a sufficient explanation for her behavior or her end. Bithia, an Egyptian, and Ruth, a Moabitess, were outsiders in Israel as well, yet they acted in the spirit of the helpmeet-opposite in a way that Jezebel never did.

The Necromancer of Endor (I Samuel 28)

There are people who, perhaps feeling that God is not interested in their daily lives, turn to other forces to try to avoid harm or to gain advantage for themselves. Ancient people widely believed in many varieties of magic and soothsaying, and in stories about demons, vampires, love potions, and more. Greeks believed in fate *(moira)* and necessity *(ananke)*. The Scripture forbids all these superstitious practices because they imply the belief that there are powers in the world other than God himself and that people need to protect themselves against evil powers and call the good ones to their aid. This detracts from the people's faith and their closeness to the true Creator, thus deflecting them from what is most important in life.

The Scripture teaches that "you shall be blameless before the Lord your God" (Deut. 18:13). People should have faith in God and not seek to influence events by magic. Witchcraft, in all its forms, was prohibited in Israel — on pain of death. It is in this context that one must understand King Saul and the necromancer as recorded in the narrative of I Samuel 28. As Israel's first king, Saul is a man of many great qualities of character, but also certain flaws. After the death of his master, the prophet Samuel, the Philistines have invaded Israel in large force. However, when Saul seeks God's advice through visions or prophets, God does not answer. Growing more and more concerned about his situation, Saul decides to seek help of another kind. He had suppressed the practice of all sorts of sorcery in his kingdom, as Hebrew law ordered; but now he asks his aides to find a necromancer — a woman who can raise the spirit of Samuel from the other world to advise him (a more recent example of this practice would be a séance).

Saul disguises himself, though it must have been difficult to disguise a man so tall and handsome, and he goes with two of his aides to Endor, where the woman lives. Her initial response to her visitors is negative. Don't they know that King Saul has stopped the practice of necromancy? Are they trying to get her executed? Saul, without revealing his identity, assures her that she will come to no harm and orders her to call up the spirit of Samuel. She performs her magic rites, and Samuel's spirit comes up, looking very authentic because he is dressed in the same sort of coat he wore during his life. Immediately, the woman realizes in the spirit's respect for Saul that he is indeed the king. Now she cries out in fear: "Why have you deceived me? You are Saul." But Saul calms her down and asks Samuel to tell him what will happen. Samuel's prophecy is indeed dire: Saul's army will be badly defeated by the Philistines, and he and his three sons will be slain. This confirms the worst of Saul's fears. He collapses to the ground, emotionally devastated by this terrifying report as well as physically exhausted after not having eaten all day.

The woman helps the king get up. "Behold," she says, "your maidservant listened to you, and I took my life in my hands and obeyed what you told me." Now she urges him to eat, and she prepares him veal and baked bread. With his strength somewhat revived, Saul goes on his way — to his own defeat and death the next day in the battle on Mount Gilboa.

Did this woman actually bring up the spirit of Samuel, or was she simply a clever fake? The matter is much debated. Some scholars say that the apparition was indeed Samuel, and others say it was merely a demon in disguise. Still others insist that the woman (apparently, the practitioners of witchcraft in the ancient world were typically women) was merely a theatrical expert who put on a good act and had a man with a gravelly voice hidden backstage to impersonate a ghost. The necromancer of Endor was an intelligent woman with some empathy for people. She certainly seems to have had Saul's best interests in mind: after his devastating prophecy from the ghost of Samuel, she revived him with a good meal, which necessitated the slaughter of her fattened calf. Yet she operated as part of a nefarious profession, one that acknowledged powers in the world other than God, and the practice needed to be stamped out: by participating in this practice, she was rejecting the one true God and his covenant and mission.

THIS STORY ACKNOWLEDGES the intuitive sensitivity of women: they often show a greater ability than men to see into the core of life and the future, and both the biblical and Greek traditions were cognizant of this. However, Greeks feared this ability in their women, while the Bible respected it. Women in Greek myth, such as Medea, use this power to bring devastation, and they are feared. The Hebrew Bible, in contrast, includes several stories of important leaders who consult wise women, including prophetesses such as Huldah and Deborah. It is not surprising that Saul turns to a woman for direction about the future; his mistake is that he does not stay within the biblical limits and instead consults a necromancer.

Yet the necromancer was very different from the witches and *maenads* of Greek myth, who were excluded from any serious role in the world by the rational thought of Greek males. These women hated the dominant order and sought to destroy it. The necromancer in I Samuel 28 shows no hatred of Saul or of the Israelite faith. She calls up the spirit of Samuel reluctantly, not out of any malice toward Saul, but in an attempt to help — albeit mistaken. If Saul had not gone to the necromancer, would he have avoided his tragic defeat? No, because God had already ordained that he and his sons would die at the hands of the Philistines. So the necromancer herself is not entirely to blame. It would have been better if she did not practice this voodoo, but she was not a ruthless or unfeeling person.

Potiphar's Wife (Genesis 39)

The biblical story of Potiphar's wife again involves an encounter not only between personalities but between widely variant cultures. The focus is on the difference between a life devoted to meaningful obligations and commitments and one that seeks gratification and freedom without commitment or the giving of self. The story also brings out contrasting views of sexuality.

In this narrative in Genesis 39, Joseph, the seventeen-year-old son of Jacob and Rachel, is put in a pit by his brothers and later taken by Midianite merchants and sold to caravan traders, who transport him to Egypt. There he is sold as a slave to Potiphar, an important government official. Very bright and capable, Joseph does well in his new environment. Successful in his work, he also maintains the moral and religious standards that his parents have inculcated in him. This is a difficult task because Egyptian life and culture at the time was very different from that of the Israelites. The Egyptians were polytheistic, worshiping a multitude of gods and fetishes in elaborate rituals and ceremonies. They had built magnificent temples and pyramids, which stand to this day as monuments of not only their religion but the glory of their architectural accomplishments. But Egyptian moral standards were far looser than those required by biblical law and practiced in Joseph's family.

Joseph has the strength to resist the temptations of his new land, and Potiphar soon recognizes both the excellence of his work and the depth of his commitment to God: "And his master saw that God was with him and that in all that he did God prospered him" (Gen. 39:3). Soon Potiphar appoints Joseph head over his entire house and estate, and again Joseph performs magnificently, so that Potiphar trusts him with all his affairs unquestioningly.

Potiphar's wife now steps onto the stage. She has noticed Joseph's abilities and, of course, his striking good looks, and she tries to seduce him. Joseph now faces a terrible dilemma: if he refuses her, she can make terrible trouble for him; but adultery is clearly against the Hebrew laws concerning sexuality: sexual activity is to be limited to the commitment of the marriage pact. Matters of sexuality were very different in Egypt; promiscuity and sexual aberration were common enough to be socially acceptable. Masters having sex with slaves was a given. Also, the prominence of eunuchs was in stark contrast to Hebrew culture, which banned eunuchs from the assembly of those practicing the faith of Abraham, Isaac, and Jacob. In this story, the wife of Potiphar may feel genuine attraction for Joseph, but to her he represents an affair, which offers some excitement but no bonding or commitment, and certainly no sanctification. Joseph can be sold or dispatched when she tires of him.

Joseph turns her down, explaining that he would never feel right in betraying Potiphar. When that does not make an impression on her, he tries to explain that adultery is forbidden by his God. Potiphar's wife is not interested in that excuse either, and she continues to press Joseph day by day, only to be rebuffed each time. One day when Joseph goes into the main house, no one is there but Potiphar's wife. Joseph may know that all the other men are away, and for a moment he may be ready to yield to temptation. Finding that she is alone with Joseph, Potiphar's wife again tries to seduce him. A Midrash says that Joseph is ready to give in when the image of his father flashes into his mind and he remembers God's purpose in building a new faith and covenant on Jacob and his family. In that moment Joseph realizes that his life has too much meaning to be cast away for a meaningless flirtation with his master's wife.

Potiphar's wife seizes hold of Joseph's jacket, but Joseph breaks away in a panic and rushes out of the house, leaving his jacket in her hand. Angry at Joseph and fearful that he may report her to her husband, Potiphar's wife plans a strategy to smear Joseph. She calls in the servants and, showing them Joseph's garment, accuses him of trying to rape her, degrading him as a Hebrew foreigner in order to win them over. When Potiphar comes home, she tells him the same story, emphasizing not only Joseph's lowly foreign origin but also his status as a slave, which she has, of course, omitted when telling her story to her other servants.

Potiphar probably knows both Joseph and his wife well enough to guess the truth of the matter, so he does not have Joseph put to death. Instead, he places him in a prison for political prisoners; there Joseph, with his great abilities and high moral stature, soon becomes the trusted aide of the chief officer. God is with Joseph in prison, too, and he is still "a successful man" (Gen. 39:2, 23). Because of his moral character and abilities — including his dream interpretations — Joseph will go on to become the viceroy of Egypt and, more important, to be reunited and reconciled with his family and to fulfill his role as a major figure in the founding of a great faith.

WHAT MAKES Potiphar's wife attempt to seduce Joseph? Is she genuinely attracted to Joseph, or does she want to dissuade him from his purpose? Does she have a sense of purpose herself, or is she using her charm in a destructive way? Does she have any sense of loyalty to Potiphar? Does their marriage have a purpose that encourages fidelity and sacrifice? Or is it merely an exercise in pointless hedonism and materialism? These are some of the many questions that emerge from this narrative of the life of Joseph and of Israel.

Recollections of his father Jacob remind Joseph of the depth of his commitment to the covenant and of the higher purpose of his life. If he were to succumb to the seduction of Potiphar's wife, he would not only betray Potiphar but ultimately himself, his family, and God. Potiphar's wife has nothing of this sense of purpose to command her loyalty, and she uses her charm in a destructive rather than a constructive way. From this point of view, we can see that her seductive nature is a failure to know herself. She cannot be a helpmeet-opposite to

Potiphar because she has no identity of her own and because her relationship with Potiphar has no transcendent purpose. And she cannot respect or even understand Joseph's rejection of her advances or his sense of loyalty and purpose because she lacks any sense of transcendent purpose for herself.

Lot's Wife (Genesis 19)

Lot's wife plays only a brief role in the Genesis story of the fiery destruction of Sodom. The biblical record does not give her a name other than "Lot's wife," but midrashic sources record her name as Idit. God has sent angels to Lot, the nephew of Abraham, to warn him that the city of Sodom, where he lives, is to be destroyed in a storm of fire and brimstone. The people of Sodom are very prosperous but act with great cruelty toward others. With the terrible doom impending, the angels hurry Lot, his wife, and his two daughters out of the city. God's instruction through the angels is: "Do not look behind you, and do not pause in the plain, but flee to the mountain lest you be smitten" (Gen. 19:17).

The destruction of Sodom and its sister cities has begun as Lot and his family are fleeing. His wife turns to look behind Lot, who is bringing up the rear, toward the city that was her home, and she is turned into a pillar of salt. Lot and his two younger daughters escape to safety. Scripture goes on to tell us that it was as a special favor to Abraham that God saved his nephew's family from destruction (19:29). Why were Lot and his family ordered not to look back as they were fleeing Sodom?

Greek mythology tells the story of Orpheus, greatest of musicians, whose new bride, Eurydice, is fatally bitten in the ankle by a snake shortly after their marriage. Orpheus makes his way down to Hades to recover her. There he so charms the ruling gods with his music that they agree to allow him to take Eurydice back to earth; the only proviso is that Orpheus may not look back after he has left Hades until he reaches his home on earth. Overjoyed, Orpheus leads Eurydice up the dark passage back to the sunlight, his music lighting their way. But just as he is about to step onto the earth's surface, he turns around to see if his beloved is still with him, and as a result she is returned to Hades. Orpheus looks back out of his love for her and anxiety that she may be losing strength: "Here, anxious in case his wife's strength be failing and eager to see her, the lover looked behind him, and straightway, Eurydice slipped back into the depths. . . . Eurydice, dying now a second time, uttered no complaint against her husband. What was there to complain of, but that she had been loved?" Orpheus cannot bring himself to remarry, and instead he turns to the love of boys (Ovid, *Metamorphoses* X, ll. 1-85).

The similarity of the main motif in the two stories seems striking. People (whether Lot or Orpheus) are not permitted to turn back to see the hell they are escaping. But closer analysis shows that the two stories impart very different messages. Lot's wife is punished because of her insufficient attachment to Lot and her inability to separate herself from Sodom. On the other hand, Eurydice is punished because her husband, Orpheus, is so deeply attached to her. Orpheus looks back not because he is attached to Hades but because he is attached to Eurydice.

Commentaries offer several ideas as to why Lot's family was commanded not to look back. The destruction of the cities was so awesome that to see it might have been harmful to them. Or, perhaps, they were not worthy of being rescued, nor morally superior to the people left in the city. Or, perhaps, the destruction was coming so close that there was not a moment to lose. Lot and his family were saved largely because of their blood kinship with Abraham and not because of their own merit. Lot's earlier behavior, in which he was willing to sacrifice his daughters to the mob gathering at his front door, does not portray a man of impressive character (see chapter 5).

Moreover, there is no indication that the Lot family members have fully separated emotionally from the city of Sodom. This was perhaps why Mrs. Lot looks back. She appears to have been part of the life of the city, a basically satisfied citizen who has not taken a stand against the city's evil ways. This is also apparently true of the older daughters, who, with their husbands, scoff at Lot's urging and decide to stay in Sodom. The heart of Mrs. Lot may still be in the city, and she may well be leaving reluctantly, not appreciating or feeling a part of the great moral drama that is being played out. In a moment of crisis, Mrs. Lot fails utterly to make the moral commitment to a faith in God and the covenant and to the support of her husband — matters that give real meaning to human life. Like Potiphar's wife in the preceding story, she appears to lack the personal identity necessary to be a full helpmeet-opposite.

The myth of Orpheus appears, at first glance, to be a charming fairy tale. More careful scrutiny, however, reveals something very troubling. Orpheus's whole purpose in descending to Hades is to bring back the new bride whom he loves so dearly. Forbidding Orpheus to look at his beloved Eurydice is an act of cruelty that expresses the gods' malevolent sense of humor and brutality that is so typical of Greek mythology. The story lacks moral content and bears instead the lesson so prevalent in mythology: people can only lose when they struggle with the caprices of fate.

THE CONTRAST BETWEEN Lot's wife and Eurydice is clearly drawn, though each is in a sense an anomaly in her own culture. From the biblical point of view, a person must leave his or her parents' home to build a family. Had Lot's wife done so, she would have left Sodom with Lot without looking back. But Mrs. Lot is enmeshed in the pagan ways of Sodom and is unable to separate from those ways. She cannot follow the angels' order not to look back because she lacks the faith and the love to do so. She does not behave in the way of Sarah, Rebecca, Rachel, and Leah, who leave their parents' homes to follow their husbands. Lot's wife seems more tied to her origins in Sodom than she is to Lot, and so she is turned into an inanimate pillar — punished for her lack of love and her lack of trust in her Creator.

Eurydice and Orpheus love each other dearly, but it is Greek mythology's sense of irony that they be punished for this. Orpheus loves Eurydice so much that he goes down to Hades to recover her, and then he cannot stand not looking at her. He cannot follow the capricious and unfeeling rules of the gods of the underworld because they are unnatural and cruel. Eurydice and Orpheus are both punished for their love rather than their lack of love.

CHAPTER 12

Accepting One's Mission

"Where there is no vision, the people perish" (Prov. 29:18). This statement emphasizes the importance of recognizing and accepting one's mission, and it applies to a number of biblical women. Tamar, for example, understands far better than does Judah, her father-in-law, the importance of her role in continuing the family of Jacob; later, Judah comes to realize this. In another story, Zipporah seems better able than her husband, Moses, to understand the importance of circumcising their son, and she does so.

The comparison of Vashti, Esther, and Zeresh in the book of Esther provides yet another example of the benefits and importance of accepting one's mission. Vashti, the wife of Emperor Ahasuerus of Persia, lacks a higher sense of mission and sinks into a foolish power struggle with her husband, in which she publicly embarrasses him and he responds by putting her to death. Zeresh is even worse: driven by ambition, she unscrupulously pushes her husband, Haman, when she thinks he will succeed, and she abandons him when his trajectory is descending. Esther behaves quite differently: brought into Ahasuerus's harem against her will, she nonetheless uses her position to influence him to save her own people after Haman has plotted to annihilate all the Jews of the realm. Rahab is an outsider, a Canaanite woman who comes to recognize the moral and spiritual superiority of Israel's faith to her own morally corrupt society, and she embraces the vision of that covenant and purpose for herself and her whole family.

Tamar of Genesis (Genesis 38)

At a very dangerous moment in the history of Jacob's family, a woman takes action in a daring and unique way to fulfill the meaning of her own life and the lives of those around her. The narrative in Genesis 37 recounts how Jacob's sons become so jealous of their brother Joseph because of the favoritism Jacob has so obviously shown to him and because of Joseph's dreams of superiority over them that they want to kill him. Reuben, who is the oldest and feels some responsibility for Joseph's safety, persuades them to throw him into a dry pit instead — thinking that he will let Joseph out and send him home when the others have moved on. But while Reuben is gone, the other brothers, led by Judah, sell Joseph to a passing caravan of Midianite traders, who carry Joseph off to Egypt and sell him as a slave. Reuben is distraught when he returns to find that Joseph has disappeared. So the other brothers realize that they have to make up a story about Joseph's fate. They dip Joseph's coat of many colors in goats' blood and bring it to Jacob, allowing him to conclude that his favorite son must have been devoured by a wild beast. Jacob mourns deeply for his brilliant and beloved son, and the whole family and their unique mission of monotheism and ethics are traumatized and imperiled. The lies of Jacob's sons initiate a pattern of deception that is difficult to break.

Judah, Jacob's fourth son, is a leader among the sons of Israel; indeed, the royal family of David and Solomon will stem from his descendants. Part of the kingly powers of his personality is the fact that he does not lie to himself and that he does step forward to accept responsibilities. It is Judah who prevents his brothers from killing Joseph; nonetheless, he convinces them to sell Joseph and deceive Jacob. Now, in Genesis 38, Judah separates himself from the society of his brothers and goes into business with Hirah the Adullamite, a local merchant. He marries a local woman, the daughter of Shua the Canaanite (that is, someone outside the family and covenant), and the couple eventually raise a family of three sons. Er, the eldest, marries a fine woman named Tamar; but God slays Er for an unspecified wickedness, and his widow is left with no children. The Hebrew levirate law required that the brother (or close relative) of the deceased marry his childless widow to try to have a son with her — a son who would be an heir to the deceased. So Judah instructs Onan, his second son, to take this responsibility with Tamar. But Onan does not want to "give seed to his brother"; pretending to consummate his legitimate (but unwanted) marriage to Tamar, he allows his seed to fall to the ground rather than produce a son to carry on his brother Er's heritage (thus the word *onanism*). Onan's behavior is displeasing to God, and like his older brother, he also dies.

Judah then tells Tamar to return to her father's house and live life as a widow while she waits for his third son, Shelah, to reach the age when he will be able to marry her and fulfill the levirate requirement. But in point of fact, Judah, seeing that his two older sons have married Tamar and died shortly thereafter, fears that he will be sending Shelah to the same fate. Time passes, and Tamar, who is no fool, realizes that Judah does not intend to send his third son to marry her; but she is determined to bear children for Er's sake — as well as to accept and participate in the God-given mission of Jacob's family.

In the meantime, Judah's wife dies (she is not named in the text, referred to only as Shua's daughter). After his period of mourning, the new widower Judah goes to Timnah with his friend and business associate Hirah for the annual shearing of the sheep, an important event that is celebrated with feasting and drinking. Tamar hears of this and is determined to practice a deception of her own, a lie whose purpose is honorable and will be, in Scripture's terms, "eye-opening." Dressed as a prostitute and with her face covered, Tamar approaches Judah at a crossroads as he is returning from the shearing. Though it is proscribed by everything in his upbringing, Judah decides to have relations with this "prostitute" and begins to negotiate a price. He offers a goat as payment for her services, but since he has no goat with him, she asks for his signet ring, his staff, and threads from his garment as a security deposit.

Tamar has deliberately chosen three items to show Judah how far he has fallen, because these items are symbolic of the authority that Judah has degraded. We should note that Tamar, in her deception of her father-in-law, is sitting at a *petach anayim*, which is generally translated as "crossroads"; but the Hebrew term, taken literally, would mean "opening of the eyes." By deceiving Judah, Tamar would open his eyes and reveal to him what was best in himself. In impregnating Tamar, Judah himself will thus beget the children (Tamar will have twins) to replace Er and Onan. (Tamar's liaison with her father-in-law was to be forbidden in later biblical law; but at this time it was a legitimate form of levirate marriage.)

Judah sends his friend Hirah back to the crossroads to give the supposed prostitute the goat for her services, and to reclaim his security deposit; but despite Hirah's search, the woman cannot be found. Judah is somewhat perturbed, but he decides to let the prostitute keep his symbolic pledge because a public search for her and his signet, staff, and cord will end up being embarrassing to him. The relationship of Judah and Hirah is interesting: Judah clearly does not hesitate to reveal his peccadilloes to Hirah or to ask his friend to cover for him.

Tamar soon begins to show signs of pregnancy, and she makes no secret of her condition. To the public eye it would appear that, while living as a widow and still bound to Shelah, Tamar has committed adultery; so she is sentenced to death. As her last moments approach, Tamar shows the ring, staff, and garment that Judah has left with her, saying "By the man to whom these belong, I am pregnant. Recognize, please, to whom belong this signet and cloth and staff." Tamar does not mention Judah by name; rather, she offers him the chance to take responsibility on his own for what he has done. And the biblical writer deliberately intends this to sound like Judah's earlier statement to Jacob when the brothers returned Joseph's bloodstained coat to him: "Recognize, please, is this your son's coat or not?" (Gen. 37:32). It is likely that Tamar is here reminding Judah of how he deceived his father.

Judah indeed recognizes the three objects as his own, and his sense of what is right pushes him to the next step: he acknowledges the unborn child as his own in a phrase that has several layers of meaning but is well translated as: "She was righteous (because I did not give her Shelah). It is by me." Pressed by Tamar, Judah has risen to take responsibility for his own acts. Tamar actually gives birth to twin sons, Perez and Zerah, Judah's only heirs, who become the ancestors of King David and his dynasty. The proof of a real change in Judah's character will show even more strongly soon after this. The remainder of Genesis (chapters 39 through 50) goes on to tell the story of Joseph's rise from slavery to become a viceroy in Egypt. When famine comes, food can be had only in Egypt, and Jacob's sons go there from Canaan to purchase supplies. Joseph's brothers do not recognize him, and he seeks to test their loyalty to each other by pretending to arrest Benjamin, the youngest. And this is the moment when Judah steps forward. He has assured his father, Jacob, that he will be responsible for Benjamin's safety, and now the moment of truth has come. Not realizing that it is his brother Joseph, Judah remonstrates with the threatening viceroy — flattering, cajoling, and appealing to his sense of decency. Finally, when nothing else seems to work, Judah offers himself as a slave to replace his youngest brother. Clearly, Judah has now taken on great responsibilities and has become the leader of his family. But it has been Tamar's wisdom and courage that has enabled Judah to find his better self and to help Jacob's family continue in its great historical mission to spiritual fulfillment.

SOMETIMES A WOMAN can see better than a man can what is important and what is not. Judah may be acting toward Tamar in a way he thinks is technically correct, applying the law of levirate marriage to have Onan — then Shelah — marry her. But Tamar's womanly need to have a child within Jacob's family is frustrated by the actions of several men: Er's wickedness leads to his death, and Onan withholds his seed from her. Finally, it becomes clear that Judah has no intention of marrying her to Shelah; but through all of this Tamar acts righteously.

Judah may fear that Tamar herself is responsible for the death of his two older sons. What is Tamar to do, given her desire to participate in the continuation of the covenant? Perhaps it is possible for her to approach Judah directly, but she may sense that he is not ready to grasp the significance of this for the covenant. Instead, she creates her one-act play as a prostitute in order to become pregnant, even at the risk of being put to death as an adulteress. This requires great faith and the belief that Judah, when confronted, will take responsibility for his actions. Much to his credit, Judah does take that responsibility: because of Tamar's cunning and insistence, he grows as a person. This is the story of a woman who uses deception not to betray a man but to bring out the best in him. Tamar is truly a helpmeet-opposite.

Zipporah (Exodus 4)

A story about Moses and Zipporah, his wife, journeying to Egypt is told in Exodus in just a few sentences, but there is little agreement among commentators as to what actually happens. What is clear is that Zipporah's quick understanding saves the day. Moses has experienced the great prophetic encounter with God at the burning bush (Exodus 3–4), where God has appointed him as the man to lead the Israelites out of their cruel bondage in Egypt. For some years now, Moses has tended the sheep of Jethro in Midian, and he has married Zipporah, Jethro's daughter. Returning from the burning bush and God's insistence that he become the leader who will rescue the Israelites from Egypt, Moses leaves his father-in-law's home and, leading his wife and their two sons on a donkey — a lonely caravan indeed — sets out to liberate his brethren from Egypt.

This small group comes to an inn, and Moses is attacked by what the text calls an "angel" (Exod. 4:24-26). Some commentators have seen this as meaning an actual angel; others have said it was a superhuman being in the form of a snake; still others have seen the entire incident, not as an actual event, but as a prophetic vision or dream. What has gone wrong with Moses? One ancient oral tradition suggests that Moses has neglected to circumcise one of his sons — either the elder one, Gershom, or the second one, newly born, because Jethro objected to circumcision. Jethro has been so hospitable and supportive of Moses that the latter does not want to oppose him in this matter. At this point, however, with Moses having accepted the mission of being God's messenger to Pharaoh and the Israelites in Egypt, his son needs to be circumcised.

Several commentators focus on Scripture's mention of the inn. What is the story trying to tell us by mentioning this detail? Does it really matter where Moses and his family spend the night? This can perhaps explain the fact that Moses, who has just experienced the great vision of the burning bush and is on a major spiritual and historic mission, seems to have forgotten his loftier focus by attending to the small details of the lodging. Such details would be fine for anyone else to attend to, but Moses should have been fully concentrating on the higher demands of his mission.

Moses then is attacked by the angel, or by an illness. It is Zipporah who understands what is needed: she herself cuts the foreskin of her son, saying to Moses, "A bridegroom of blood you are to me." Whatever has attacked Moses releases its grip. Zipporah realizes — and Moses must now grasp the concept as well — that Moses' mission will give him little opportunity for a normal family life. She and the boys return to Midian while Moses goes on to Egypt and sets in motion the great events of the Exodus.

It is Zipporah who understands and apparently accepts her role as the wife of a great spiritual leader, someone who would come closer to God and do more for his people than any other human being. Zipporah stays in Midian and only rejoins Moses many months later, when the Israelites approach Mount Sinai to receive the Ten Commandments.

A BIBLICAL WOMAN often needs to act in a crisis when her husband, no matter how great, cannot. Zipporah responds to the angel's attack with a sense of immediacy, while Moses seems unable to act. Both Western thought and modern psychiatry can sometimes term this ability hysterical and a signal of emotional flightiness and instability — and, as such, devalue, ignore, or even fear it. In contrast, the Bible and biblical men appreciate a woman's sense of immediacy, which can often salvage a situation when a man is unable to act quickly and directly enough.

Why hasn't Moses circumcised the child himself? Perhaps it is because he has not wanted to offend Jethro. But we should note that Moses' inability to act continues after the "angel" comes; it is Zipporah who circumcises the boy and rescues Moses. The biblical narrative sometimes teaches that men may not be as good as women are at perceiving some immediate situations and doing what has to be done.

Esther, Vashti, and Zeresh (Book of Esther)

The book of Esther never mentions God's name, yet God's quiet presence behind the scenes is no less sure. Ahasuerus ruled the great Persian Empire, which consisted of 127 provinces that stretched all the way from India to Ethiopia. He gave a magnificent feast to show off his almost limitless wealth and glory — a party that was decorated lavishly and lubricated with unending wines served in a great variety of precious goblets. It is hardly unexpected for men at an extravagant drinking party, sooner or later, to begin talking about women. And when the Persian king became "merry with wine," he ordered his eunuchs to bring out Vashti, his queen, so that he could show off her beauty to his princes and officers. How drunk was Ahasuerus? Perhaps not as far gone as some of his companions: the text simply says he was "merry," not totally besotted.

He was proud of his beautiful queen, but what happens next exposes a weak link in their relationship. Vashti sees herself as a queen, a woman of status and dignity — not the kind of woman who would, to use a modern idiom, jump out of a cake, scantily clad, to entertain a collection of partying drunks. She knows that the men are "merry with wine," so she refuses to follow the king's order and satisfy his vanity, emphasizing that she is "*Queen* Vashti" (Esther 1:12) and that she will not go with the king's eunuchs or obey his order. Besides, she is serving as the hostess of her own separate party of women in the palace.

It appears that there is a long-standing debate between husband and wife as to which of them really comes from more royal stock. After demonstrating his imperial power and wealth in this grandiose feast, Ahasuerus now wishes to show his authority over his wife as well; but in choosing this way to do it, he is making a fool of himself. He realizes that he has acted badly in sending her such an insulting command, but what is he to do now? Turning to his leading advisors, the king asks what the law would dictate for Vashti, who has disobeyed the order that the king's eunuchs have brought her. It is probable that Ahasuerus still is fond of Vashti, and his question acknowledges that he has insulted her with his demands.

Can he, in some way, pardon Vashti and keep her without losing face? Memuchan, one of the Seven Advisors, speaks up: the king must make an example of Vashti, he argues. The people will not realize that the king has acted foolishly and that Vashti is not wrong to refuse him. They will believe that Vashti has deliberately snubbed the king and all his glory — not only the king but all the princes and the people of the realm. Law and order in the entire empire will be disrupted, Memuchan declares, and people will feel little obligated to obey the laws. Women, especially, will point to Vashti as a role model for not obeying or supporting their husbands (1:18: "There will be humiliation and conflict"). The king must have Vashti executed, he says, and then must send out a decree ordering women to obey their husbands as a matter of law, not merely of good will. Stealing a page from King Henry VIII's book, therefore, Ahasuerus has Vashti put to death.

Looking for a new queen, the king has the beautiful women of his realm rounded up and brought to his harem so that he can try each one for a night. Among these is a young Israelite woman named Esther, a Judean of good character who has been raised by her cousin, Mordecai, a councilor at the royal court. Esther does not ask for the perfumes and oils and fine clothes that the other women take to prepare for their night with the king. But Esther has a genuine warmth, and she "found favor in the eyes of all who saw her" (2:15).

Ahasuerus falls in love with Esther and makes her his queen. Perhaps he is tired of all the ambitious women who hope to become queen by looking and behaving like movie stars. Through all of this, Mordecai has stayed as close to matters as he possibly can — to keep tabs on what is happening to Esther. At the same time, Mordecai has done two things that have profoundly different results. He reveals to Esther the plans of two eunuchs to assassinate King Ahasuerus (and Esther informs the king, thus saving him from the plot). And Mordecai refuses to bow or pay homage to the newly promoted super-prince Haman; his faith in and worship of the one God prohibit him from doing so. This leads the vainglorious Haman to make a terrible threat: he obtains the king's consent to annihilate all the Jews of the Persian Empire. Up to this point Esther has never told the king of her origins.

Mordecai warns Esther through intermediaries of Haman's genocidal plot and urges her to go to the king. But Esther hesitates for fear that the king will not accept her petition, and that this will bring disaster on her and her people. Mordecai, however, understands the need for immediate action and tells Esther that she cannot remain silent. God will save his people, he says, if not through her then through someone else (4:13-14). Mordecai portrays for Esther the dramatic opportunity before her: "For who knows whether you have been raised to the throne for such a time as this?" Esther realizes that Mordecai is right, and she appeals successfully to the king, bringing about the fall and execution of Haman, the promotion of Mordecai to the second most powerful position in the kingdom, and the rescue of her people.

IN THIS SAME BOOK of the Bible we encounter one of Scripture's most unsavory couples: Haman and Zeresh. Haman is a man who demands constant attention and adulation. When Mordecai does not kowtow enough to please Haman, the latter becomes very upset and calls together all his supporters and his wife, Zeresh. Haman recites all his honors and then says that "none of this means anything" as long as Mordecai will not bow to him. It is Zeresh who comes up with a wonderful idea: build a gallows fifty cubits high (about seventy-five feet) for Mordecai; surely the king will agree to the hanging, and then Haman can go with an easy feeling to the private party that Queen Esther is giving for the king and Haman alone. Zeresh is as heartless as Haman is: she feels that she has power and can rid herself of enemies in the most high-handed manner.

However, as is so often true in the book of Esther, events and re-versals come about unexpectedly and suddenly. That very day, the king remembers that he needs to reward Mordecai for foiling the plot on his life; and it is at this moment that Haman enters the palace to ask Ahasuerus's consent to hang Mordecai. Instead, Ahasuerus sends Haman out to lead Mordecai through the city wearing the king's cloth-ing and riding his horse, with Haman proclaiming, "So shall be done to the man whom the king desires to honor." Haman returns home deeply depressed and humiliated at the collapse of his plans, and again he calls on Zeresh and his friends for advice and support.

We have seen how women of the Bible can be strong, wise, and supportive. Zeresh is not of this mold. She comes to Haman, not with his friends but with astrologers, and, based on their views, she predicts that Mordecai will totally destroy Haman. She offers neither advice nor kindness to the frightened Haman, and she will not fight for him. It is as though she is abandoning ship at the first sign of trouble.

The king's messengers come to hurry Haman to his second ban-quet with the king and queen, one that he must now be anticipating with a certain sense of dread. At this second banquet Esther reveals Haman's cold and malicious plot to destroy all the Judeans along with Mordecai. In a rage, the king orders that Haman be hanged that very day on the same gallows he has had built to hang Mordecai. Scripture does not mention Zeresh again, but it does record that ten of Haman's sons were also hanged some months later for their part in the plan to wipe out the Judeans. Not every villain receives his or her just deserts, but Haman's case is clearly one where he does.

WHAT IF Ahasuerus and Vashti had been king and queen of ancient Ju-dah rather than Persia? First, Ahasuerus would not have given such a ridiculous drinking party. Second, he would not have demanded that his wife behave like a stripper in public. Third, Vashti would have made clear her refusal without humiliating him. Finally, her husband, the king, would certainly not have had her executed.

Such is the difference between biblical and nonbiblical women. Vashti's reaction to her husband's demand is easily understandable, but the cultural context turns a minor issue into a test of wills and egos that ends in disaster. Vashti expresses her reluctance to demean herself in a way that demeans her husband. He strikes back by executing her. Vashti does not act like a helpmeet-opposite, nor does Ahasuerus allow her to.

Note how differently Esther approaches Ahasuerus: she presents to him the problem of her people and their need for his support in a way that makes it easy for him to listen and respond to her. Basically a shy person, Esther realizes that she has been placed in a critical historical moment, and she rises to the occasion. She appreciates her life purpose, and she is able to act with a determination that may have been previously foreign to her. And she does this without antagonizing Ahasuerus, as Vashti has. Her warmth and biblical character enable her to be a helpmeet-opposite even to this rough man, and to enlist his power into her larger purpose.

The side story of Haman and Zeresh in this larger story of Esther illustrates a mistake many men make in judging their wives. A man can be drawn to an ambitious woman who seems to stand up vigorously for him by opposing his opponents in matters of politics or business or family; such a woman can sometimes entice a man because she seems to be uncompromising in these matters as she urges him to be unyielding and even merciless in achieving his aims. Compared to a woman who is gentler in nature and less partisan in judgments, the ambitious Zeresh type can be heady stuff. As the Haman-Zeresh story indicates, however, such a perception can be dangerously mistaken. Zeresh supports Haman not because she loves him, but for her own gain. At the hint of a reversal or failure for Haman, Zeresh is gone. The ruthless and unfeeling attitude she has shown toward Mordecai turns against Haman himself in the end.

Rahab (Joshua 2)

The second chapter of the book of Joshua recounts the story of Rahab, another of the remarkable biblical women whose clear vision and courage enable her to see through a difficult situation and make a wise and important decision. The story begins a few weeks after the death of Moses, and Joshua now leads the Israelites, who are poised to cross over the Jordan River to begin the conquest of Canaan, the "promised land" of Israel. Joshua sends two men on an intelligence mission: they are to spy on as much of the land as they can, and especially Jericho, the fortress city that will be the gateway to the whole. Rather than stay in the relative safety of the countryside, the spies enter Jericho itself, seeking to get some sense of the mood of the people. They go into the establishment of Rahab, who seems to be running a business something like the saloon of the Old West — a combination bar, restaurant, hotel, and perhaps brothel. Many people are coming and going, and the men from Israel see it as a good place to gather local talk and information. A woman of experience and savvy, Rahab probably quickly perceives that the two strangers are Israelites.

Facing the threat of attack by the Israelites, about whom they have heard rumors, the people of Jericho are tense; they watch strangers carefully. It is soon reported to the king that two Israelite men have been spotted in town, and he sends a message to Rahab that she must bring the men out — because they are spies. Rahab has sized up the situation and the timing carefully, and decides for herself that the future lies with God and the people of Israel. She tells the king's messengers that two men have indeed visited but that they left her house and Jericho just before the city gates closed at dusk. She claims not to know where they are headed; but, she says, they cannot have gone far, and if the king's men were to pursue quickly, they could surely overtake them. The king's men go out in pursuit of the spies, but Rahab has, in fact, hidden them under piles of flax that are drying on her roof.

With the king's men safely gone, Rahab goes up to the roof. The text does not say how she has first learned who the spies are, but she is clearly an astute and perceptive women. She tells the men that she realizes that God has given the land to the Israelites, and that the Canaanites are melting with fear before them. "For we have heard how God dried up the Red Sea before you when you left Egypt and how you obliterated Sihon and Og, the two Amorite kings across the

Jordan. We heard and our hearts were crushed, and no man's spirit can rise against you. For the Lord your God is God of heaven above and earth below" (Josh. 2:10-11).

Rahab indicates in this last sentence the depth of her understanding and her acceptance of the biblical conception of God as a deity who rules and precedes both spirit and nature, and who watches over his earth and people. This contrasts sharply with the nature-bound religion of the Canaanites. Rahab also rejects any abstract conception of a deity who is too lofty to be concerned with earthly matters. Rahab portrays the situation very clearly. Even today we can sense in her words the terrible fear of the people of Jericho as they feel the power of the approaching invasion. Remarkably, though, Rahab seems to be the only one who knows what to do. The king of Jericho will fight and will lead his city to destruction. But Rahab embraces a new truth and a new people.

The spies express their indebtedness to her for saving them, and they swear to spare any member of her family who will remain in her house during the battle, including her parents and siblings and their families. There is no mention that Rahab has a husband, and this may support the idea that Rahab is a prostitute or a madam. They arrange that all she has to do is hang a scarlet cord from her window so that the Israelite soldiers will be able to identify her house and not destroy it. At this moment, since her house is built into the city wall, Rahab lets the spies down from a window with a rope, and they escape to the hills, where they remain for several days — until they believe that the search parties from Jericho have given up the pursuit.

Their report to Joshua reflects their purpose: it is not a study of enemy fortifications or troop dispositions, but it merely states that "God has given all the land into our hands and all the inhabitants of the land are breaking down before us" (Josh. 2:24). Rahab and her family do come through the spectacular destruction of Jericho safely, and later sources claim that Rahab would join the nation of Israel and that some very distinguished progeny would descend from her, including the prophet Jeremiah.

ALTHOUGH IN ONE SENSE Rahab betrays her own city, she is not simply an opportunist trying to advance herself. She has recognized God. Unlike Lot's wife, she separates herself clearly from a community that is not only going to be defeated by a superior military force but is already defeated spiritually. Rahab understands this and does not hesitate to rearrange her priorities and accept a new outlook.

We should emphasize again Rahab's description of the Israelite God as the "God of heaven above and earth below" (Josh. 2:10-11). Canaanite society was morally corrupt, and the Israelites were the covenant bearers of a vital new faith that was neither nature-bound nor overly abstract. The biblical God who created heaven and earth also created each individual human being in his image and cared about that person's life on the earth. It is important for a woman to recognize and accept her mission, because if she does so, her life will have a purpose that is defined not simply by the men in her life but more in terms of finding her place in God's plan for history. Rahab has the intelligence and wisdom to perceive the spiritual as well as the political meaning of the momentous events surrounding her home and her city, and she has the courage to follow her mission by casting her lot with the God of Israel.

Miriam's Song (Exodus 15:20-21)

After the Israelites experience the crossing of the Red Sea, Moses leads them in a great song of praise to God: "Then Moses and the children of Israel sang this song to God, and they said . . ." (Exod. 15:1). Verses 14-15 relate that all the nations of their then-known world stand in awe of this immense event. The song enumerates the many things God has done in leading the Israelites out of Egypt, concluding with a pledge of faith that "God will rule forever and ever" (15:18). Miriam, the prophetess and sister of Moses and Aaron, realizes that a woman's voice is missing in this paean to God. She takes a timbrel in her hand and leads the women out after her with timbrels and with dances. Her song is musical and to the point: "Sing to the Lord, for he is exalted. The horse and its rider he has thrown into the sea."

Although Moses' song is lofty, it lacks the musicality, movement, and indeed the spirit that Miriam and the women can contribute. In a sense, Miriam and the women provide a bridge between Moses' grand sense of faith and that of life itself. Indeed, in several places the Bible associates music with the spirit of prophecy.

WOMEN'S VOICES are different from men's, but they are just as real and just as important. Women's music can bring liveliness, creativity, and distinctiveness to a grand but sometimes stilted form of expression. Biblical women intrinsically express the quality of being givers of life, and thus they are in some ways more attuned to the world than are men — and less prone to camouflage their praise in lofty theories and concepts. Moses' song consists of a profound praise to God: it is very conceptual and enumerates all the things God has done to aid the Israelites' exodus from Egypt. Miriam's song goes right to the point, and she animates her praise of God with dance and music. Men can sometimes be long-winded, while women are more likely to go directly to the point.

Epilogue

In this book we have presented about fifty stories concerned with how biblical women have dealt with life situations — from the quiet and modest to the highly dangerous and dramatic. These stories can be used by laypeople, but also by clergymen and counselors, to understand personal problems and growth that show a continuity between those ancient narratives and life today. Modern psychology has tended to look to Greek mythology rather than biblical foundation stories as its basis for understanding and helping people. This can be seen in the central role that psychoanalysis gives to the classical Greek story of Oedipus and his father, Laius, rather than the biblical story of Abraham and Isaac. Similarly, C. G. Jung has focused on the Electra complex for women as a "feminine Oedipus complex." But what would be the implications for modern psychological health and growth of focusing on the biblical story of Naomi and Ruth rather than the Greek story of Electra and her mother, Clytemnestra?

Isaac, Circumcision, and a
Resolution of the Oedipus Complex

Let us begin with a brief summary of the story of Oedipus and how it has given us the "Oedipus complex." King Laius of Thebes is warned by an oracle that there will be danger to his throne and his life if his newborn son is allowed to reach adulthood (this is a common theme in the ancient world, and also occurs in the biblical narrative: see, for example, the treachery of David's son Absalom in II Samuel 14 and after). So Laius gives the child to a common herdsman with orders to destroy the child. The herdsman, after piercing the infant's feet, cannot bring himself to kill him and instead gives him to a fellow shepherd, who in turn takes the child to King Polybus of Corinth and his queen, who adopt him and call him Oedipus, or "swollen-foot."

Many years later, Oedipus, who has learned from an oracle that he is destined to be the death of his father, leaves the kingdom of Polybus, because Polybus is the only father he has ever known. It happens, of course, that King Laius, Oedipus's biological father, is at that same time driving to Delphi, accompanied by two attendants. They meet Oedipus on a narrow road, a quarrel breaks out, and Oedipus kills both Laius and his attendants. Shortly after this event, Oedipus saves Thebes from the sphinx, a monster that is part woman, part lion, and part eagle, a being who has been devouring everyone who cannot guess her riddle. In gratitude for their deliverance, the Thebans make Oedipus their king and give him their recently widowed queen in marriage. Oedipus has already become the unwitting killer of his father; now, in marrying the queen, he becomes the unwitting husband of his mother.

As described by Sigmund Freud, the Oedipus complex represents an archetypal dilemma for the son within a family. The Oedipal son wishes to replace his father and have his mother to himself: "King Oedipus, who slew his father Laius and wedded his mother Jocasta, is nothing more or less than a wish-fulfillment, the fulfillment of the wish of our childhood."[1] According to classic psychoanalytic con-

---

1. Sigmund Freud, *The Interpretation of Dreams* (London: Hogarth Press, 1954), p. 296.

cepts, the father counters the son's threat to displace him by threatening to castrate the son. This serves to neutralize rather than resolve the son's desire to displace the father, which results in a mutual standoff in the father-son relationship, a fear-based identification of the boy with his father, and a fear-based superego.[2] The son gives up his desire to possess his mother; he may, in fact, displace the fear of castration from his father to his mother. In the process of then identifying with his father, the son may come to regard his mother as a seductress and see her sexuality as lethal.

In his call for a biblical psychology, Erich Wellisch has offered the Akedah (Abraham's obedience to God in binding his son, but his ultimate non-sacrifice of Isaac) as an alternative to the myth of Oedipus.[3] For Wellisch, the biblical story and its covenant of love offer an unambivalent resolution of the father-son relationship that replaces the cold peace between father and son that emerges out of the incomplete resolution of the Oedipus complex. The narrative of Abraham's binding of Isaac is in Genesis 22: first, God calls on Abraham to offer his only son, Isaac, as a sacrifice (Gen. 22:2); second, Abraham seems prepared to go through with the sacrifice, saying to Isaac that God will provide a lamb for the sacrifice; at the same time, Isaac trusts God and his father (22:6-8); finally, God sends an angel at the last moment to command Abraham not to sacrifice Isaac, and Abraham sacrifices a ram instead (22:9-12).

Wellisch argues that this Akedah experience produces an actual modification of instincts:

> A fundamental effect of Abraham's change of outlook was the realization that God demanded life and not death. Abraham realized that the meaning of the commanded sacrifice was not to kill his son but to dedicate himself and his son to lifelong service to God. He completely rejected the former dominance of his

2. Freud, *The Infantile Genital Organizations: An Interpolation into the Theory of Sexuality* (London: Hogarth Press, 1923a, 1923b, 1924).

3. Erich Wellisch, *Isaac and Oedipus: Studies in Biblical Psychology of the Sacrifice of Isaac* (London: Routledge and Kegan Paul, 1954).

death instinct and entirely abandoned his aggressive tendencies against Isaac. His life instinct was tremendously promoted and with it a new love emerged in him for Isaac, which became the crowning experience of his religion.[4]

Wellisch is saying something truly radical here: this experience encourages "instinct modification" in the attitudes of fathers toward sons, and vice versa. It is not surprising that Wellisch's view has been severely criticized in psychoanalytic circles, because it mixes "religion" with "psychology." Even someone as sympathetic to Wellisch as Theodore Reik has viewed Wellisch's claim for a modification of instincts in the Akedah experience as a psychological impossibility.[5]

However, a closer reading of the biblical account suggests that Wellisch's analysis may be correct but that it is incomplete in that it fails to explain the concrete mechanism by which the "instinct modification" may come about — covenantal circumcision. God says to Abraham: "And as for you, you shall keep my covenant, you and your seed after you throughout their generations. This is my covenant, which you shall keep, between me and you and your seed after you, every male among you shall be circumcised. And you shall be circumcised in the flesh of your foreskin: and it shall be the token of a covenant between me and you" (Gen. 17:9-11).

Consider again the Freudian resolution of the Oedipus complex that Wellisch sees as incomplete. The son threatens to displace his father, and this taking over his father's power is symbolized by his possession of the mother. The father threatens castration in response. The ambivalent neutralization of the Oedipus complex available to Greek society may be seen as a cold war between these two forces: the threat of displacement balanced by a threat of castration. Covenantal circumcision provides for a modification of the entire familial situation. The father knows that the son will inherit the covenant and thus will not try to displace him (the father); the son knows that the father could have

---

4. Wellisch, *Isaac and Oedipus*, p. 89.
5. Theodore Reik, *The Temptation* (New York: Braziller, 1961), p. 225.

castrated him but did not. Instead, circumcision becomes the very symbol of the son's right of inheritance and right to his own life.[6]

What is important is that it is the merging of the physical and spiritual domains that provides the dynamic for the biblical transformation of the father-son relationship described in the Akedah story. The father knows that the son is not motivated to displace him because the son knows he will be his father's inheritor; nor is the father's identity threatened by the son. Indeed, he wants to see his son develop and surpass him. Circumcision addresses directly the son's fear of castration by representing a sanctified, benevolent substitute. Covenantal circumcision actually transforms the son's primordial fear into his very assurance that the father's own interests lie in the son's being fit to carry on the covenant. The two generations have a vested interest in each other's well-being. The son wants a teacher, and the father wants an heir. Circumcision is a concrete physical act that internalizes this spiritual transformation and provides an unambivalent resolution for the father-son relationship unavailable in the Greek world and most of the Western world's literature.

Ruth, Ritual Purity, and a Resolution of the Electra Complex

A similar argument can be made with regard to daughters. Biblical stories can provide a resolution of the Electra complex that was unavailable in Greek narratives. Euripides depicts Electra, daughter of Agamemnon, as waiting for years, completely obsessed with her plans for the return of her brother, Orestes, and their revenge on their mother, Clytemnestra, for her murder of her husband and their father, Agamemnon. Raised by both mother and father to see herself as debased in her womanhood, Electra is hostile toward both her mother and men in general, as well as toward her own lowly role. She is married to a farmer from a good family, "one of a noble nature"; yet Electra treats

6. Kalman J. Kaplan, "Isaac and Oedipus: A re-examination of the father-son relationship," *Judaism* 39 (1990): 73-81.

him poorly and boasts to strangers that she is still a virgin. Plotting to murder Clytemnestra, Electra tells her mother that she has just had a baby. When Clytemnestra arrives, Electra lets out her long-cherished hostility in a lengthy speech, accusing her mother of cuckolding Agamemnon. Clytemnestra's response to her daughter is insightful concerning Electra's preference for her father over her mother: "Daughter, 'twas ever thy nature to love thy father. This too one finds; some sons cling to their father, others have deeper affection for their mother." Although Electra (with the help of Orestes) murders her mother rather than killing herself, her reaction further displays her essential feeling of debasement as a woman: "Ah me! alas! and whither can I go? What share have I henceforth in dance or marriage rite? What husband will accept me as his bride?"

The Electra complex is a term proposed by Jung for the Freudian concept of the "feminine Oedipus attitude" in young girls. According to Freud, the daughter, like the son, is originally attached to the mother; however, she discovers that she lacks a penis, and thus she feels inferior to the male. She becomes angry at her mother because she holds her responsible for her condition. As a result, she turns her libidinal attachment onto the father and imagines that she will become pregnant by him. She believes that the pregnancy will replace the missing penis, because of which she envies males, and will allow her to gain equal status with the father.

This argument is less convincing than the one underlying the Oedipus complex. Menstruation troubles and humiliates a woman more than any imagined lack of genitalia; it may cause her to feel impure and envious of males.[7] And it may result in a daughter's willingness to abandon her mother and to look to her father. The mother's defense is to lower her daughter's self-esteem by eliciting even further shame about the latter's menstruation and femininity, making it risky for the daughter to fully abandon her mother, lest she wind up totally alone — without either mother or father. Such an action on the part of the mother results in the daughter's feeling worse about herself than

7. Cf. William N. Stephens, *The Oedipus Complex* (New York: Free Press, 1962).

she did before. The attachment between Greek mother and daughter is permeated with a symbiotic and suicidal quality, leaving the daughter unable to cope in a healthy way with the stresses of life. The mother neutralizes her daughter's threat of abandonment by provoking in her a shame of menstruation.

As we have argued above (pp. 110-14), the biblical story of Naomi and Ruth provides a very different view of mother-daughter relationships: it is a story that integrates commitment as well as independence. Naomi bolsters rather than attacks Ruth's self-esteem; Ruth, in turn, refuses to abandon Naomi and shows a beautiful loyalty to her. Unlike Clytemnestra, Naomi does not try to bind her daughters-in-law to her, but unselfishly urges them to go back to their original homes to find husbands. She recognizes that they have a right to their own lives, that they are not simply objects to serve her. This caring reciprocity continues throughout the story: Naomi continuously encourages and helps Ruth to fulfill her own needs, and Ruth embraces Naomi and includes her in her eventual happy home with Boaz. In the biblical model the emphasis shifts from competition between mother and daughter to a united effort toward fulfilling the covenant. The parents teach children as a fulfillment of the covenant, and the children honor the parents as an aspect of obedience to God — not simply personal obligation to parents.

The daughter's role in the biblical world differs from the son's, but it is highly important. A woman's sexuality is accepted as normal, not as a cause for shame. Menstruation does not cause diminution in self-esteem, as it does in many pagan societies. Biblical culture and requirements transform this bodily process into part of the woman's unique gift: it is the woman's task to observe carefully the laws that govern and sanctify the physical aspects of her womanhood. The essential biblical law and practice is that a woman and man avoid sexual contact during her menstruation. At the appropriate time, after the termination of her menstrual flow, she may cleanse herself in the ritual water, after which full sexual contact between husband and wife may be resumed. The virgin-whore dichotomy is absent, and woman's sexuality is not feared. Furthermore, a daughter need not abandon her mother in order to possess her father and thus achieve security. Likewise, a mother need not evoke in her daughter a shame of menstruation. In the biblical model a girl is not treated as an expendable object but as a person with her own sense of purpose and an unconditional value to her existence.

This covenantal structure also overcomes the daughter's fear that her father will abandon her when she leads her own life. Leaving her parents' house to become a wife and mother on her own is a joyous and sacred fulfillment of her duty as a woman of valor. The Midrash recounts that, when Rabban Gamaliel's daughter was getting married, he blessed her in this way: "May you never return to my house, and may the word 'woe' never depart from your mouth." He then explained: "May you be so happy with your husband that you have no need to return to your parents' home; and have children and be devoted to raising them well" (Genesis Rabbah 26:4).

The biblical husband honors and respects his wife; she, in turn, helps to pass on the covenant. Her role as a mother is to guide her children on the path to finding spiritual, emotional, and material fulfillment with God. Essential to this is the daughter's acceptance of her feminine nature without shame. The daughter does not need to abandon her mother in order to ally with her father (thus resolving the Electra dilemma); instead, she accepts nurturance and learning from her mother without being symbiotically connected to her. It is this assurance of nurturance that allows the daughter to be a daughter. The daughter neither fears abandonment by her father nor desires to fuse with him. She can come to trust that her father will recognize her sense of purpose and not to use her for his own interests, and she allows him to teach her.

The mother knows that her daughter is a partner in the tradition, that she does not need to abandon her mother; and the daughter knows that her mother does not need to evoke shame in her. The father's transformation in the family is pivotal: he is transformed from child exposer to child protector, resolving the daughter's Electra complex and strengthening her hold on life. Parents can thus relate in a truly nurturing manner to their daughter and to each other, and they provide genuine protection for their daughter and support her need for healthy development. She is able to love without becoming enmeshed.

Central to this biblical view of woman is that she is a helpmeet-opposite, a full personality who is essential to the divine plan for the world. She must express her own opinions and desires in her relationship with her mate, not out of fear of attachment or a search for false independence but as a carrier of the divine purpose and as a full partner in God's plan for creation. The Bible's purposive view of parent-child relationships provides the basis for a health-oriented psychology rather than one that is centered on simply understanding and resolving classical, primordial conflicts. Both mother and father can contribute much toward the health of their children: "Hear, my child, the instruction of your father and do not forget the teaching of your mother." Parents teach by direct instruction, example, empathy, support, and correction. Mother and father share in transmitting to the child a sense of commitment and of the child's unique preciousness in God's plan for history.

The essence of child-rearing aims not merely at resolving the primal conflicts but at establishing a pattern of ongoing learning. Conflict resolution is not a final goal in itself, though it may support necessary stages of human growth. More deeply, it is learning both through intellect and behavior that fosters real change and growth and the serious ability to overcome one's feelings of fear, guilt, or inadequacy. Both parents contribute to their sons' and daughters' learning, and many biblical stories — as well as later commentaries and interpretations — tell of the positive interaction of parents and children. The Fifth Commandment says: "Honor your father and mother." The Bible often emphasizes the recognition and respect that the young must pay to their elders — for example, "You shall rise before a gray head, and you shall honor the face of the aged." But the elders and parents, too, must understand their great responsibility with regard to passing on God's covenant commands and promises to their children: "You shall teach them diligently to your children, and [you] shall talk of them when you sit in your house, when you walk by the way, when you lie down, and when you rise up" (Deut. 6:7).

Conclusion

In this book we have tried to focus on the immense potential and responsibility the biblical woman has in fulfilling the various roles given to her — be it within the household as daughter, wife, and mother, or in the larger context of helping to fulfill God's plan for history. We began this book with a discussion of six largely unfulfilled women who are well-known characters in Western literature. These women often found their lives drab and pointless, and having a sense of commitment to God's purpose in history might have helped them find meaning in their own lives.

Flaubert's Emma Bovary, for example, is bored with her physician husband and child and the small town where she lives. She fills her life with sordid flirtations in which she fruitlessly attempts to escape boredom and loneliness. Why doesn't she seek fulfillment by helping her physician husband care for the sick and by creating an atmosphere of purpose and service in which to raise her child?

Ibsen's Nora is infantilized by her husband and not allowed to express her considerable individual creativity within their marriage — either as a wife or as a mother. Instead, she feels the need to fly away to find the freedom to express herself, thus ironically becoming the "little skylark" her husband has pejoratively labeled her.

Tolstoy's Anna Karenina is charming and smart, but her beauty does not call forth a sense of giving that could invigorate her life, nor does it help her find a true partner with whom she can share a meaningful life.

Chekhov's Anna has contempt for her much older husband, whom she has married to salvage her own dysfunctional family of origin; but her behavior also displays contempt for herself. The marriage may have been one of necessity and ultimately unsuitable for her, but she compromises her own dignity and purpose in her abusive treatment of her husband.

Edith Wharton describes Lily Barth as a beautiful and intelligent woman who is preoccupied with re-establishing her place in high society. She pursues flirtations with a number of wealthy men, passing up the possibility of a deep relationship with one man who truly loves her. Lily lacks the biblical sense of a true marriage, that is, being part of a larger meaning structure with a transcendent purpose.

Warm and lively, Fontane's Effi Briest would probably have been better off marrying someone more suitable than the older and strait-laced man she married. However, given that she did not, she still could have expressed herself in ways that were more constructive than having a risky affair that proves to be destructive for both her lover and herself — and indeed her child. Even though, like Effi, a woman may have a husband who is very different from her, she can still find and even create meaning in a marriage with such a mate by understanding and living by God's plan. From a biblical perspective, the ultimate success of a marriage is based on the couple's acceptance of God as the third partner in the marriage — because it is God who underwrites the entire process.

This book describes an alternative model for women to those found in Greek mythology and much of modern fiction and drama. It is her very sense of being a full participant in the divine plan for the world that *frees* the biblical woman to fully develop as a human being and as a partner. The helpmeet-opposite that is organic to the biblical concept of woman from the time of the very first woman, Eve, is a woman of purpose who finds fulfillment and meaning in expressing her personality in constructive achievements and relationships.

Bibliography

Abarbanel, Isaac. *Perush*. (Hebrew) 6 volumes. Jerusalem, 1964.

Alter, Robert. *The David Story*. New York: W. W. Norton, 1999.

Aschkenasy, Nechama. *Women at the Window: Biblical Tales of Oppression and Escape*. Detroit: Wayne State University Press, 1998.

Babylonian Talmud. New York: Art Scroll, 2006.

The Bible. Authorized King James Version. Oxford: Oxford University Press, 1997.

Burkert, Walter. *Homo Necans*. Berkeley, CA: The University of California Press, 1983.

——— . *The Orientalizing Revolution: Near Eastern Influence on Greek Culture in the Early Archaic Age*. Cambridge, MA: Harvard University Press, 1994.

———. *Babylon, Memphis, Persepolis*. Cambridge, MA: Harvard University Press, 2004.

Chekhov, Anthon. "Anna on the Neck." In *The Duel and Other Stories*. Mineola, NY: Dover Publishing Company, 2003.

Dalley, Stephanie. *Myths from Mesopotamia*. New York: Oxford University Press, 2000.

Eisemann, Moshe. *Iyov*. New York: Mesorah Publishing Company, 1994.

Esquivel, Laura. *Like Water for Chocolate*. Translated by C. and T. Christensen. New York: Doubleday, 1992.

Flaubert, Gustave. *Madame Bovary*. New York: Chelsea Publishing Company, 1998.

Fontane, Theodore. *Effi Briest*. New York: Ungar Publishing Company, 1966.

Freud, Sigmund. *The Ego and the Id.* [Standard edition of Complete Works of Sigmund Freud.] *Volume 19,* 12-59. Edited and translatd by J. Riviere. London: Hogarth Press, 1923a.

———. *The Infantile Genital Organizations: An Interpolation into the Theory of Sexuality.* In Standard Edition of the Complete Works of Sigmund Freud, *19,* 12-59. Edited and translated by J. Strachey. London: Hogarth Press, 1923b.

———. *The Interpretation of Dreams.* In Standard Edition of the Complete Works of Sigmund Freud, 4 and *5,* 12-59. Edited and translated by J. Strachey. London: Hogarth Press, 1954.

Graves, Robert. *The Greek Myths.* 2 volumes. Baltimore: Penguin Books, 1955.

Graves, Robert, and Raphael Patai. *Hebrew Myths: The Book of Genesis.* New York: McGraw-Hill Company, 1963.

Herczeg, Y. *Rashi.* Brooklyn, NY: Art Scroll, 1995-99.

Hesiod. *Works and Days* and *Theogony.* Translated by Stanley Lombardo. Indianapolis: Hackett, 1993.

Hirsch, Samson R. *Pentateuch.* Translated by Isaac Levy. 6 volumes. Gateshead, UK: Judaica Press, 1976.

———. *Psalms.* Translated by Gertrude Hirshler. New York: Feldheim, 1978.

Holy Scriptures. 2 volumes. Philadelphia: Jewish Publication Society of America, 1917.

Homer. *The Iliad.* Translated by Richmond Lattimore. Chicago: University of Chicago Press, 1951.

———. *The Odyssey.* Translated by Richmond Lattimore. New York: Harper and Row, 1967.

Ibsen, Henrik. *Four Great Plays: A Doll's House, The Wild Duck, Hedda Gabler, The Master Builder.* New York: Pocket Books, 2005.

Kaplan, Kalman J. "Isaac and Oedipus: A re-examination of the father-son relationship." *Judaism* 39 (1990): 73-81.

———. *TILT: Teaching Individuals to Live Together.* Philadelphia: Brunner/Mazel, 1988.

Kaplan, Kalman J., and Matthew B. Schwartz. *A Psychology of Hope: An Antidote to the Suicidal Pathology of Western Civiliation.* Westport, CT: Praeger, 1993.

———. *The Seven Habits of the Good Life: How the Biblical Virtues Free Us from the Seven Deadly Sins.* Lanham, MD: Rowman and Littlefield Publishers, 2006.

Kaplan, Kalman J., Matthew B. Schwartz, and Moriah Markus-Kaplan. *The*

Family: Biblical and Psychological Foundations. New York: Human Sciences Press, 1984.

Kirk, Geoffrey, and J. E. Raven. *The Pre-Socratic Philosophers*. Cambridge, UK: Cambridge University Press, 1971.

Lefkowitz, Mary. *Heroines and Hysterics*. London: Duckworth, 1981.

Lefkowitz, Mary, and Maureen Fant. *Women's Lives in Greece and Rome: A Source Book in Translation*. Baltimore: Johns Hopkins University Press, 1992.

Leibowitz, Nechama. *Studies*. Translated by Aryeh Newman. Jerusalem: The Jewish Agency, 1981.

Malbim, M. L. *Otzar Haperushim*. Jerusalem, 1956.

Midrash Rabbah. 2 volumes. (Hebrew) Jerusalem, 1971.

Oates, Whitney J., and Eugene O'Neill, Jr., eds. and trans. *The Complete Greek Drama, Volumes 1 and 2*. New York: Random House, 1938.

Ovid. *Metamorphoses*. Translated by Rolphe Humphries. Bloomington, IN: Indiana University Press, 1967.

Plato, *Apology and Phaedo*. Translated by Harold N. Fowler. Cambridge, MA: Harvard University Press, 1971.

———. *Republic*. Translated by Desmond Lee. Middlesex, UK: Penguin Classics, 1983.

———. *Symposium*. In *The Portable Plato*. Translated by Benjamin Jowett. New York: Viking, 1959.

Plutarch. *Plutarch's Lives*. Translated by John Dryden. New York: Modern Library, 1975.

Pomeroy, Sarah. *Goddesses, Whores, Wives and Slaves: Women in Classical Antiquity*. New York: Schocken, 1975.

———. *Spartan Women*. New York: Oxford University Press, 1975.

Pritchard, James. *Ancient Near Eastern Texts*. Princeton, NJ: Princeton University Press, 1955.

Ramban. *Commentary on the Torah*. Translated by Charles Chavel. New York: Shiloh Press, 1971.

Reik, Theodore. *The Temptation*. New York: Braziller, 1961.

Schwartz, Matthew B., and Kalman J. Kaplan. *Biblical Stories for Psychotherapy and Counseling: A Sourcebook*. Binghamton, NY: The Haworth Pastoral Press, 2004.

Shestov, Lev. *Athens and Jerusalem*. New York: Simon and Schuster, 1966.

Simon, Bennett. *Mind and Madness in Ancient Greece: The Classical Roots of Modern Psychiatry*. Ithaca, NY: Cornell University Press, 1978.

Slater, Philip. *The Glory of Hera: Greek Mythology and the Greek Family*. Boston: Beacon Press, 1968.

Bibliography

Soloveitchik, Joseph B. *Family Redeemed: Essays on Family Relationships.* Edited by David Shatz and Joel Wolowelsky. Hoboken, NJ: KTAV Publishing House, 2002.

Stephens, William N. *The Oedipus Complex.* New York: Free Press, 1962.

Tolstoy, Leo. *Anna Karenina.* New York: Chelsea Publishing Company, 1987.

Twain, Mark. *The Diaries of Adam and Eve.* New York: Oxford University Press, 1986.

Wellisch, Erich. *Isaac and Oedipus: Studies in Biblical Psychology of the Sacrifice of Isaac.* London: Routledge and Kegan Paul, 1954.

Wharton, Edith. *House of Mirth.* New York: Vantage Press, 1990.

Yerushalmi, Yosef H. *Freud's Moses: Judaism, Terminable and Interminable.* New Haven: Yale University Press, 1991.

Zornberg, Aviva. *The Beginning of Desire: Reflections on Genesis.* New York: Doubleday, 1996.

Index

Index

Index